Gotta Ballroom

East Dunbartonshire Council

Contents

DVD Menu

Total running time: 64 minutes

Preface

So, you've decided you want to learn to dance. Maybe you've been to a wedding and the dancers seem to be having so much fun. Or perhaps you want more exercise, and dancing looks like a fun way to do that. It might be a great way to spend more time with your partner. Or you just saw a ballroom dance competition on TV and thought, "I just have to do that." There are probably almost as many reasons to learn to dance as there are people who want to learn. Each of us has our own motive. But whatever your reasons, learning to dance can be a wonderful experience.

The purpose of this book is to make learning to dance fun and easy. Most people agree that watching good dancers moving effortlessly to the music can be mesmerizing. And once you get a taste of it, dancing can be addictive, as many of us have found out! In this book, which is part of the Gotta Dance series, you will learn four American style (or "American smooth") ballroom dances: waltz, tango, foxtrot, and Viennese waltz. These dances move around the floor and are characterized by a flowing and free style of movement. Also included in the book for your enjoyment are a number of interesting quotes about dancing.

This book consists of three sections: Part I, Getting Into Ballroom Dancing, exposes you to background information about dancing in general—the history, trends, and music. Chapter 1, The Changing Face of Ballroom Dance, explains dance trends that have been influenced and shaped by cultural shifts. Chapter 2, Dancing as a Hobby, explores dancing as an art, a sport, and a social activity. This chapter helps you to understand your goals in dancing and some of the different roles that dancing fills in society. Chapter 3, Connecting Music and Dance, will help you learn to recognize the music for each of the four ballroom dances.

Part II, Learning Ballroom Dancing, covers basic terminology, step patterns, and combinations for the four ballroom dances. Chapter 4, Posture and Movement, shows you correct dance posture and how to move gracefully. You will learn how to use your feet properly to make the dances flow. You'll also learn the directions for moving around the floor through the use of a diagram. Chapter 5, Two People Dancing as One, explains what makes a good leader and a good follower. This chapter also explains the various dance positions and turning techniques. The information in chapters 4 and 5 will lay the foundation for your understanding of the four dances in this book. Chapter 6, American Style Waltz; chapter 7, American Style Tango; chapter 8, American Style Foxtrot; and chapter 9, American Style Viennese Waltz include the characteristics of each of these dances and basic step patterns to get you moving around the floor with ease. Throughout the chapters are explanations of how each step fits into that dance style and when and how to choose that step. Also included are several combinations of all the step patterns.

Part III, Ballroom Dancing on Your Own, provides your chance to try what you've learned. When you go to your first dance, you will be completely on your own. There will be different music than what you're used to. The dance floor will be a different size and shape from what you've been practicing on. And the biggest change, there will be many people on the floor, some trying to dance for the first time, too. Chapter 10, Surviving the Social Dance Floor, shows you how to cope with problems that may arise during your first few times dancing in public. You'll learn how to ask strangers for a dance and even how to turn down a partner if you really aren't interested in dancing at that time. You'll also learn dance etiquette and tips on proper dance attire and proper grooming. Chapter 11, Taking Your Dancing to the Next Level, provides information about private and group lessons and practice parties. It also describes the different levels of dance to help you determine the type of dancer you want to become. Terms often heard to describe dancers are bronze, silver, and gold. This chapter sheds light on what those levels mean to you, the dancer. This chapter also describes the two styles of dance: American and international. The reasons for learning each style are explored so you can decide which you would like to learn.

A lot of information is included in this book, but the combination of the book and DVD will make your learning easier and more complete. The first two chapters are informational. If you are interested in history and how dancing has developed over the years, then begin reading with chapter 1. You may be surprised to see how partner dancing has evolved through time. Even if you want to get right into the actual dancing, you should at least read chapter 2 first to learn more about the dancer you want to be. Learning about yourself and your motives will make the learning experience more comfortable. Chapters 3, 4, and 5 are technique and reference chapters. You will have to refer to them as you go through the dance patterns to get the positions, music, and footwork correct. Each dance chapter (chapters 6 through 9) describes the step patterns in detail. It's best to go slowly and learn just the foot positions and footwork first. After you feel comfortable with the actual step patterns, add the styling and characteristics of each dance. Go slowly. Don't try to do everything at once! Take your time to fully understand each element, then add new elements one at a time. Before moving to the next pattern, review the previous patterns.

The temptation may be to stay with one dance all the way through, then move to the next dance. However, most beginning dancers make better progress by learning the first few patterns in each dance and then going back to add more step patterns. This allows you to build a strong foundation in the basics before moving on to more advanced patterns. Each dance has elements that are used in the others, so learning all the dances together is beneficial. Also, when you go out dancing, if you have studied only one dance, you will sit out most of the evening. But if you have learned a few basic patterns in each of the dances, you can dance the whole night if you want, even while still learning!

This book and DVD are designed for you to use together to maximize your learning. The DVD includes demonstrations of most of the practice exercises and all of the step patterns in the book. Each exercise and step pattern that is demonstrated on the DVD is noted in the book for quick and easy reference! However, please note that some of the material is presented in a different order on the DVD than in the book. This occurs because the demonstrations on the DVD are performed in dance position, so, logically, dance technique must be presented first (in the book, dance position isn't discussed until chapter 5). To avoid confusion when navigating the DVD, please use the menu to locate the desired supplementary section. Remember, it's best to move at your own pace; don't feel you have to rush. Everyone has a different rate of learning and retention. Refer to the book and DVD as often as you need to. And don't forget to go back and review!

Gotta Ballroom will start you on the road to a whole new world—the wonderful world of ballroom dance. An added bonus is a resource section in the back of the book showing you where to go for more information on dance lessons, dance opportunities, costumes, and anything mentioned in this book. The resource section provides a plethora of information to keep you moving on your dancing journey. So, let's get dancing!

PART

1

Getting Into Ballroom Dancing

The Changing Face of Ballroom Dance

Partner dancing has evolved through the ages and has certainly been influenced by many factors: etiquette, politics, economics, social mores, and even fashion! Knowing where we came from allows us to better understand where we are now and perhaps even gives us a glimpse of where we may be headed. Styles are cyclical, and what was popular yesterday may be popular again tomorrow. The same can be said of dancing. History repeats itself, and so does dance. Although it's doubtful that we will return to the dance styles of the Renaissance, we can see some of the influences on the ballroom dances of today and how history has brought us to where we are now. At the very least, we can look back and smile a little at the past. This chapter outlines the historical, social, and political factors that helped shape ballroom dance as it is today. It also focuses on the media trends of the United States in the twentieth and twenty-first centuries and how they have affected American partner dancing.

ROOTS OF PARTNER DANCING

A look into history can trace modern partner dancing back to the Renaissance. The Renaissance, which means rebirth, refers to the social and artistic movement in Europe from the late fifteenth century to the early seventeenth century. It was a time of revisiting the beauty and artistry of ancient Greece and Rome; this resurgence was demonstrated in art. Until this time, people acted however they wanted to: spitting and belching in public, blowing their noses anywhere they chose, and shouting abuses at each other (similar to what we see at a sporting event!). But then, personal styles of nobility and the upper classes were studied, and books of etiquette began to appear. Beauty, refinement, and civilized manners were revered, and this was also reflected in the dances of the day.

During this historical period, social dancing was identified as court dancing because it was danced by members of the royal court. Dance masters employed by nobility created and taught the dances. The couples moved together in a sequential and choreographed pattern, much like a formation, so there was little room for individual expression because everyone did most of the dances together in groups. The dances mirrored the strict social etiquette and how men and women behaved in that era. Polite, cordial, civilized—that was the order of the day, and the dances were created to exemplify those ideals. The movements were refined and exact. The dances of the Renaissance emphasized the dancers' feet more than their bodies. The clothing of the times most likely dictated that. Bulky and restrictive clothing was the fashion—ruffs around the neck, tight lacing for men, corsets for women—which did not allow for much head, arm, and upper-body movement.

Renaissance dance is a broad term covering a large spectrum of dances from all over Europe and spanning nearly two centuries. The dance masters traveled around the continent and began to study the dances of the commoners, and they integrated some of their movements into the court dances. Even though the clothing could be restrictive, the dancers still enjoyed energetic movements, such as leaps, jumps, and hops. The movements imbued their dancing with the sense of social freedom and frivolity that the lower classes possessed. In fact, French aristocratic ladies sometimes built mock villages on their palatial grounds so they could "play like the peasants." They wanted to escape from the tightly controlled dictates of nobility, even if it was just for an afternoon of fun. That trend was also mirrored in the dances of the times. At the same time, while the upper classes were dancing steps extrapolated from the lower classes, the lower classes emulated and copied the aristocracy!

> Let us read and let us dance—two amusements that will never do any harm to the world.
>
> *Voltaire, eighteenth-century French writer and philosopher*

The baroque dances were part of the next movement, emerging in France in the early seventeenth century. Even though the dances of the Renaissance were still widely practiced, the new style was spreading throughout Europe. The art of the baroque period was extremely elaborate and ornamented, and so were the dances. One of the longest-enduring dances introduced during that time was the minuet, a dance in 3/4 time. A dignified couple dance derived from a French country dance, it was introduced in 1650 at the court of Louis XIV. Small steps, stylized bows and curtsies, and graceful and precise glides were de rigueur in the minuet, and the beautiful music of the period exemplified that. The minuet thrived and became the most popular dance well into the eighteenth century. During the baroque period, almost everyone danced: peasants, nobility, and servants. In fact, it was a social requirement that one know certain dances because they were practiced at social functions, meetings, and so on. If people didn't know the dances, they were unable to attend. That, of course, made the dance masters happy because it kept them in business choreographing and teaching the dances.

Toward the end of the 1600s, a major shift in dance began. Until that time, the same basic techniques were employed both by dancers at social events and by professional dancers in theatrical productions. But now, the dance masters, seeking to maintain refinement, dignified behavior, and control of the dance, developed the five basic foot positions and used exaggerated turnout of the feet. That development gave birth to classical ballet. For the first time, a difference in dancing for performance and dancing as a social activity emerged.

Around 1690, the landler was being danced in Austria, and sometime around 1720 it gained popularity in Germany and Switzerland. The name *landler* comes from the word *land* and roughly means coming from the countryside. It was a heavy-footed folk dance in 3/4 time and is thought to be a likely predecessor to what we now know as the waltz. Animated hopping, slapping, and stamping steps with complicated underarm turns were the key elements of the dance, not the smooth and flowing elements that we expect of a waltz today. People who moved to Vienna took the landler with them, and because of new, smoother dance floors and improved shoes for dancing (no more hobnailed shoes!), they were able to dance the steps more quickly and smoothly. The faster version of the landler evolved into what we now call the Viennese waltz.

It's debatable as to whether the landler was truly the earliest ancestor of the waltz. Some say the volta is the earliest version of what has become the modern waltz. The volta (which means turning) was an Italian court dance in 3/4 time first introduced in 1556. Another incarnation is the allemande figure that was danced in the middle of the eighteenth century in the contradanse (a French development of English country dancing). Couples turned while holding each other at the shoulders. It soon became popular and became a dance on its own. It was the first time that a couple took a closed dance hold for an extended period. Until then, most of the dances were done side by side or in an open position, not face to face and so close.

And so the first true waltz was born around 1750. It was a whirling dance and was so named from the German word *waltzen*, which means to revolve. The couples danced close together with the man's arm around the lady's waist, which was shocking behavior for the time. That dance hold was considered an embrace among polite society. Men and women simply did not touch each other that closely in public. The waltz was also intriguing because the couple danced as an independent pair and not in a formation. It was also objected to as a health hazard because the dancers quickly whirled around the room. Even though the waltz was simple and unsophisticated compared to the stately court dances, the upper classes couldn't let the lower classes have all the fun, so they happily joined in.

The dance masters, of course, objected to the waltz. The dignified and complicated dances of the court were being put aside for the simpler dance form. Here was a dance that did not require lengthy instruction from the dance masters. The steps of the waltz were easy to grasp compared to the laborious and technically difficult court dances, such as the minuet. The dance masters were losing control, and not only of the dancing. They had always been the chaperones of society, and social functions revolved around them. They ran the social functions: setting up the events for the evening, starting the dances and calling out the dance patterns, and creating and teaching the dances. But now, couples were breaking away, actually starting the dance on their own and not dancing in a formation. The dance masters felt threatened. People were enjoying a sense of liberation, and they certainly expressed it through the waltz. Toward the end of the French Revolution in 1799, more than 600 dance halls had sprouted in Paris alone. After the French Revolution, Austria became the focal point of European musical and literary culture. The Viennese waltz was now being danced all over Europe.

The first appearance of the waltz in America was in 1834, when Lorenzo Papanti gave an exhibition hosted by a Boston socialite. The dance, much slower than the very fast Viennese waltz, became known as the Boston, after its American debut city. The Boston was the first dance to be performed with parallel feet. Because the feet were not turned out, as they were in ballet and the court dances, it was easier for people to dance it. The response in America was the same as in Europe. Although many people enjoyed the new dance in 3/4 time, the religious and social leaders thought the dance much too sexual in nature as dancers moved closer together. Sometimes even their cheeks touched! Of course, the younger generation was all for that and enthusiastically embraced the waltz and each other.

> The waltz is a dance of quite too loose a character, and unmarried ladies should refrain from it altogether, both in public and private; very young married ladies, however, may be allowed to waltz in private balls, if it is very seldom, and with persons of their acquaintance. It is indispensable for them to acquit themselves with dignity and modesty.
>
> *Mme. Celnart,* The Gentleman and Lady's Book of Politeness, *Boston, 1833*

More partner dances came about as a result of the growing popularity of the waltz. The polka, which was originally created in Czechoslovakia in 1822 and introduced to France and England in 1843 and subsequently to the United States, was the second closed-couple partner dance to gain popularity.

The mid-1800s (and continuing into the end of the century) are generally referred to as the Age of Reform. Labor laws changed, and the middle class suddenly had more leisure time. The first National Woman's Rights Convention was held in Worcester, Massachusetts, in 1850. The abolition of slavery was also a major event in U.S. history. People wanted to escape, to celebrate, and to dance. And they did. By 1850, the waltz reached a newfound popularity and became the most popular dance of the century. Composers created exquisite waltz music as Europe and America were being swept away by the beautiful and romantic dance. Johann Strauss and Josef Lanner kept Austria, and indeed all of Europe and the United States, twirling in fast 3/4 time to strains of beautiful Viennese waltzes. By 1900, waltzes made up three-quarters of a social dance event. The remaining quarter was made up of all the other dances combined.

The scandalous waltz was the catalyst for turning dancing into a romantic social activity. Couples were dancing together for fun, and they were enjoying their freedom to dance outside of a formation. The music was beautiful and exciting, and couples were touching each other and looking into each other's eyes while whirling around the room. Partner dancing had forever been changed.

Until that time, the emphasis on dance in the United States had been imported English country dances and other European dances. Toward the end of the nineteenth century, however, Americans were enjoying a wave of patriotism, with the end of the Spanish-American War in 1898. When American composer John Philip Sousa wrote the "Washington Post March" in 1889, it became the perfect music for the two-step, the newest dance to spread through the United States and then Europe. During that period, he wrote stirring marches that inspired people to dance to the rousing music. Not flowing like the waltz, the two-step consisted of a series of chasses, forward or sideways, with a skip in each step. Elements of the original two-step remain in today's foxtrot and quickstep. Waltz, polka, and two-step were the dances of the gay 1890s, and America was dancing into a new century.

INFLUENCE OF MUSIC AND MEDIA ON PARTNER DANCING

Dancing and music were influenced as the United States and the societal mores continued to change throughout the twentieth century. The Great Depression, Prohibition, the women's movement, two world wars, immigration, social and racial tension, the automobile, and television all influenced how Americans lived and how they danced. The country was evolving at a breakneck pace and no longer relied on dance trends from Europe. In fact, Europeans were beginning to look toward the United States for their new dances. In 1906, Sir Reginald St. Johnston wrote in *A History of Dancing*, "It is certain that our American cousins are fonder of dancing than we are, and it is to them we must look for any new dances." American composers were creating music that Americans (and indeed immigrants coming into the country) could interpret to make their own dance styles. A dance revolution exploded and paved the way for our dances of today.

1900 to 1919: Ragtime

In the first decades of the 1900s, Americans were becoming bored with the music and dances of their grandparents. They were ready for the new century to bring about great changes. In the past, trends in music and dancing had usually come from the upper echelons of society, but the young people of the day found themselves drawn to the new ragtime music of the rural South and Midwest. Ragtime music, which had begun to develop in the late 1890s, suddenly was being thrust to the forefront. Ragtime had an intoxicating feel: a rhythmic conflict between its steady march beat pitted against an eccentric, syncopated melody above. This type of music was full of life, and the young people in the United States embraced its vigor completely. Ragtime coincided with the new dance craze of the 1910s. The United States was emerging as a world leader, and not by accident. Europe was now importing the latest music and dances from the States instead of the other way around. Immigrants were flocking to the United States, bringing their own music and customs. From 1910 to 1914, more than 100 new dances emerged. However, few of those dances, even though they were fun to do, contributed much to the art of dance. Dances with animal names—bunny hug, grizzly bear, monkey glide, chicken scratch, and turkey trot—were the rage. Most of them were simple to the point of awkwardness. The turkey trot, for instance, consisted of fast marching to the beat of the music while pumping the arms at the side and then periodically flapping the arms like a crazed turkey.

That era began a time of new and exciting cultural freedom for women in society and on the dance floor. The women's suffrage movement was at high speed, racing toward the ratification of the Nineteenth Amendment in 1920, finally giving women the right to vote. During that time, women demanded that their voices be heard and that they be seen as equals to men. More women were being educated, seeking jobs in traditionally male-dominated fields, even getting involved in politics. They also wanted to be able to relax and have fun like men did. Some of the aforementioned animal dances involved acrobatic tricks and perilous dance positions. The women were losing control on the dance floor in order to enjoy their dancing and prove that they were able to keep up with the men. No more did they want to be demure, retiring creatures like their grandmothers. And good or bad, the men realized that they needed the women as partners to make the dances work. The older members of the dance community did not like the energetic dances and the freedom that the dances created. The cultural leaders and social reformers were firmly against what they called the sensuous nature of its dances and their low origins. They did not like that the dances had roots in a society they thought was unsavory, namely the black culture and the association with bars and brothels. They believed that the corrupting influence had to be abolished to save their children. Legislation was pushed to outlaw certain dance steps, even to outlaw ragtime music. But those measures were not entirely effective. Where there's a will, as it has often been said, there's a way. And America's youth was quite willful. A subtler "weapon" had to be found to combat what was deemed to be unseemly behavior on the dance floor.

During that time, show dance couples became popular at the dance halls. Show dance couples were dancers who performed exhibitions to promote dancing. One of the couples was Vernon and Irene Castle. They came along at the perfect time and were the perfect couple to appease people on both sides of the dance fence. Their show contained a tasteful portrayal of each dance that was more in tune with the wishes of the older, more conservative members of society. But they were also a young, attractive couple, which made them and their style appealing to the younger generation. Elisabeth "Bessie" Marbury, a celebrated literary and theatrical agent, saw their cabaret act and was pleased with the way they had brought refinement to the animal dances. Miss Marbury, who was a proponent of ballroom dancing for health and enjoyment, decided that the young, attractive, wholesome married couple could be the catalyst to defend dancing to those who found it vulgar and corrupting. Here was a couple that danced to the music of the day with grace and decorum, but still conveyed an air of fun and romance. She used her influence in society to make the Castles the media darlings of the decade, and they achieved fame, adoration, and acclaim much like our pop stars of today. Across from the Ritz-Carlton Hotel in New York City, they opened Castle House, a dancing school and club catering to the elite society of the city. A similar establishment, Castles-by-the-Sea in Long Beach, New York, was next, followed by Castles-in-the-Air, a nightclub atop the Forty-Fourth Street Theatre, and a cabaret called Sans Souci, also in Manhattan. They toured the country, demonstrating the "correct" way to dance. They dropped the animal dances and invented many of their own.

Around 1910, an exciting and sensual dance with Argentinean influences was becoming popular in Paris and soon spread all over Europe. Danced in seedy bars and bordellos in Buenos Aires, tango dancers had an immediate intimacy from the moment they assumed the dance hold. The woman danced in the crook of the man's right arm while she placed her right hand on the man's left hip near his pocket, perhaps looking for payment for the dance. They moved in small circles around the floor in a tight chest-to-chest embrace. The Castles (who had performed in Parisian nightclubs) are said to have brought the dance to the United States. They toned down the sensual elements so it could be danced in a socially acceptable manner and modified it so it could be taught like traditional smooth dances. The tango had been tamed, and America latched on to the dance whose popularity soared into the 1920s.

In 1914, the world was at war and the United States was again ready for change. The Castles continued to dazzle America, and Americans wanted to emulate their style. When Irene bobbed her hair, American women did as well. When she stopped wearing corsets in favor of simple, loose fitting dresses because they were easier to dance in, a new fashion wave began. Their influence on American dance (and culture) was indeed profound. Irene exemplified what women were fighting for: She was an equal partner with her husband both in business and the home. Vernon set the tone for the sophisticated gentleman. Together, Vernon and Irene Castle made dancing interesting and accessible to almost everyone. It is said that they may have invented the foxtrot, but even if they didn't invent it, they certainly helped to make it well known to society. It was known as the Castle walk when they performed it. The Castles influenced ballroom dancing until Vernon's untimely death in a plane crash in 1918.

A more likely originator of the foxtrot was Harry Fox. In 1913, Mr. Fox danced Fox's trot in his vaudeville routine, and eventually, it is said, it became known simply as the foxtrot. The actual fox may be what gave the dance its name as well. The fox has an unusual gait, walking with its feet under its body and forming a single track of footprints. The original foxtrot was danced in that manner, with the left and right feet placed directly in front of or behind the other. It wasn't until later that the foxtrot evolved to each foot having its own track on the floor. Whatever the origin, the foxtrot is one dance with an animal name that has endured. The smooth and easy movement around the floor makes it one of the most popular couple dances ever.

1920s: Jazz Age

With the end of World War I in 1918, there came another change in the United States. That was a time when Americans were in pursuit of pleasure and personal enjoyment after the misery of the war years. Henry Ford's "Tin Lizzie" made people mobile. They could drive greater distances to go dancing. Prohibition was passed, but it clearly had the opposite intended effect. People seemed more determined to seek out fun, and the younger generation was more defiant of authority. Women now had the vote, and they were ready to exercise their new rise in society and go out to have as much fun as the men did. Consequently, hemlines rose. During the Roaring 20s, young women who wore baggy dresses that exposed their arms and their legs from the knees down, bobbed their hair, smoked cigarettes, and drank cocktails were known as flappers. The name seems to have come from the way they flapped their

© Getty Images

The Savoy Ballroom in Harlem, one of the first racially integrated dance halls in the United States, was the birthplace of some of the biggest dance trends of the twenties and thirties.

arms and walked like birds while dancing the Charleston. They exemplified the modern woman. The young women of that time offended the older generation because they defied the conventions of proper feminine behavior and dared to be their own women. The Charleston was an exciting and exuberant dance with origins in South Carolina and African American styles and was introduced to the public in the Ziegfeld Follies of 1923 by the all-black cast of a show called *Runnin' Wild*. As the most popular dance of the decade, the Charleston was danced alone, with a partner, and in groups. Dance halls held Charleston contests as the dance swept the nation. Speakeasies were popping up all over. By 1925 there were more than 100,000 in New York City alone. The term *speakeasy* comes from a patron's manner of ordering alcohol without raising suspicion: a bartender would tell a patron to be quiet and speak easy. The speakeasy transcended socioeconomic barriers. People of all walks rubbed elbows with each other.

Thousands of African Americans were leaving the South and heading north to escape the problems of racism and to seek better jobs. That was called the great migration and was peaking in the 1920s. Along with them, they brought their culture, and New York City saw the start of the Harlem Renaissance. Ragtime had started evolving into the new jazz music, which had elements of West African and Western music traditions. The legendary Savoy Ballroom opened its doors in 1926 right in the middle of Harlem. During a time of racial strife, the Savoy, with its block-long dance floor and raised double bandstand, was one of the first integrated public places in America. Everyone came to hear and dance to the finest bands in a place that became a breeding ground for some of the biggest dance trends of the twenties and thirties. The Lindy hop, inspired by Charles Lindbergh's historic solo transatlantic flight in May of 1927, was first danced there before it spread across the nation. Two styles developed: One style used intricate footwork, spins, and floor steps, while the other featured acrobatic aerial movements. Other popular dances of the twenties included the black bottom and the shimmy, which involved a rapid shaking of the hips and shoulders.

One of the first bandleaders to achieve national fame was Fletcher Henderson, who formed a band in the early 1920s. Originally, his band played waltzes and foxtrots, but as jazz and blues rhythms increased in popularity, those styles became more prominent in his band's music. By the time the band took over at Roseland Ballroom in New York City and featured Louis Armstrong on trumpet, it had become a jazz band.

As America went dance crazy, dance marathons were all the rage and continued well into the 1930s. Breaking records and stretching the levels of human endurance were the craze and included flagpole sitting, mountain climbing, and aviation. But dance marathons became hugely popular because they happened in one place and also had the elements of movement and variety. They were also the equivalent of today's TV reality shows, combining real-life and theatricalized drama. They usually included some sort of staged incident, like a fight, or included couples that were professional dancers to draw a larger paying crowd. More than dancing, marathons were really about endurance. They went on for days, weeks, even months. Slower music was usually played, with intermittent faster tunes, called sprints. Judges watched to make sure that contestants, vying for fame (however fleeting) and fortune, did not allow their knees to touch the floor. Generally, the major rule was that one could not fall asleep, but some marathons allowed one partner to sleep as long as he or she was held up by and stayed in contact with the other partner. Rest times were built into the dance marathons, but the longer the marathon continued, the shorter the rest periods became. The longest-running dance marathon lasted 22 weeks and three and a half days. Dance marathons were eventually outlawed because they were unhealthy. Some people even died trying to outlast their competitors.

The new jazz music and dances were not popular with everyone. Some people called the new style decadent and dangerous. In 1921, Anne Shaw Faulkner published an article in *Ladies Home Journal* titled "Does Jazz Put the Sin in Syncopation?" Ms. Faulkner wrote, "Never before have such outrageous dances been permitted in private as well as public ballrooms." As the Charleston gained popularity, some more conservative ballrooms discouraged the dance and posted signs that read, "PCQ" (Please Charleston Quietly).

© Corbis

Marathon dancers went to great lengths to outlast their competitors as demonstrated by half-sleeping dancers in a 1924 Washington DC marathon.

1930s and 1940s: Great Depression and World War II

America's Great Depression is generally believed to have begun with the stock market crash in 1929. The initial crash was on October 24, 1929, known as Black Thursday. Five days later, on October 29, Black Tuesday was the crash that caused general panic. During the next few years there were small ups and downs, and by 1933, the economy reached rock bottom. Between 1929 and 1932 the yearly income of the average American family was reduced by about 40 percent, from $2,300 to $1,500. Banks were failing and businesses were closing, leaving more than 15 million Americans (one-quarter of the workforce) unemployed. If the 1920s were a time of excess and spending, the 1930s were anything but. Consequently, like other businesses, dancing venues were closing all over the country. Money was scarce, and people had to do what they could to make their lives happy. People looked to inexpensive leisure pursuits. Movies, parlor games, and board games became popular.

The radio turned out to be a welcomed treat. By 1939, approximately 80 percent of the population of the United States owned a radio. Comedians such as Jack Benny, Amos and Andy, and George Burns and Gracie Allen entertained radio audiences. Franklin Roosevelt used the medium for his "fireside chats," and people gathered around the radio to listen to broadcasts of sporting events, such as Yankees games. But what about dancing? With fewer dancing venues, and even less money to go to them, people tuned in to radio broadcasts of dance music and danced at home in their living rooms and parlors. "Cutting a rug" became a popular expression in American vocabulary.

By the mid-1920s, the popularity of big band dance music was already on the rise. These early big bands usually included a string section and performances were generally free of improvisation; however, by the late-1920s that style would change as bands began to embrace the idea of improvised soloing. As the big band sound shuffled into the 1930s, many bands dropped their string sections and started featuring arrangements that put improvisational playing in the spotlight. From these roots, swing music emerged in the early 1930s, and by the second half of the decade, its massive popularity would help to seal big band's place in popular music history. At the height of the big band boom, which lasted into the mid-1940s, bandleaders and musicians were as idolized as rock stars are today. A few of the most popular names of the era included clarinetist Benny Goodman, trombonist Tommy Dorsey, trombonist and arranger Glenn Miller, pianist and composer Duke Ellington, and pianist Count Basie. Their music was swing, and the dance was the jitterbug, a descendant of the Lindy. The name jitterbug came into use in the 1930s and became an all-encompassing term for various types of swing dancing. One possible originator of the name is Cab Calloway, a popular bandleader. He looked at the dancers' fast and bouncy movements to swing music and reportedly said, "They look like a bunch of jitterbugs out there on the floor."

At a time right after the stock market crash, and when the depression was at its worst, movies (especially big, lavish Hollywood musicals) provided inexpensive relief. It was perfect timing for those movies; people needed fantasy and hope in their lives. Partner dancing was portrayed as romance, and into the picture came legendary dance couple Fred Astaire and Ginger Rogers. Fred and Ginger were the epitome of grace and poise on the big screen and, quite possibly, the most famous dancing duo ever paired. Their ingenious showing of moods and emotions created magic. Astaire was not handsome by conventional Hollywood standards but was beauty in motion when he danced. Rogers was sexy with a tongue-in-cheek humor. They complemented each other perfectly. Fred appeared to glide and float effortlessly, and every woman dreamed of dancing with him. Ginger was the essence of femininity, and every woman wanted to be her. Their style was inspirational, and after their appearance together in their first film, *Flying Down to Rio*, the public demanded more. They danced in 10 films and took ballroom dancing to people everywhere. Each film contained at least one new social dance, a love duet, a competitive tap routine, and a tap solo for Fred. In *Flying Down to Rio*, the dance introduced was the carioca, where couples danced with their foreheads touching. After the film's enormous public appeal, an unsuccessful attempt was made to turn the carioca into a new social dance. Dancers found it awkward and difficult to learn without lessons and feared looking silly. Other dances introduced in their films included the continental and the piccolino. Many of their

dances were charming foxtrot-based dances, and dance teachers across America simplified them so they could teach them to a general public eager to share in the glamour of Fred and Ginger. Their ninth film was *The Story of Vernon and Irene Castle*, a tribute to the famous pre-World War I dance couple. As influential as the Castles were in their day, Fred and Ginger reached an even larger audience because of the technological advances of the media. Their films were enormous successes around the world and live on today. Fred did eventually partner with many other women in film, including Leslie Caron, Cyd Charisse, Judy Garland, and Vera-Ellen.

Other dance couples that made an impact with their

Astaire and Rogers reached an even larger audience than the legendary couple they portrayed in *The Story of Vernon and Irene Castle* due to the huge increase in the popularity of movies during the Depression era.

dancing on film in the thirties and forties include Frank Veloz and Yolanda Casazza, often billed as Veloz and Yolanda. They appeared in several films and created dances such as the cobra tango and Veolanda, and later hosted *The Veloz and Yolanda Hour* on television for several years. The DeMarcos were another dance couple that entertained film audiences during that era. The DeMarcos were actually Tony DeMarco and one of eight dance partners (three of which he married) during his career. The two with whom he achieved the most acclaim were probably Renee (Leblanc) DeMarco and Sally (Craven) DeMarco.

As much as Fred Astaire exemplified glamour on the big screen, Gene Kelly's style was down to earth and downright athletic. Instead of donning white tie and tails, Gene Kelly's look was more casual and everyday, so the viewer could easily relate to him. The 2002 documentary *Gene Kelly: Anatomy of a Dancer* featured a classic Gene Kelly quote from archive footage. He said: "I didn't want to move or act like a rich man. I wanted to dance in a pair of jeans. I wanted to dance like the man in the streets." Although he was not affiliated with one long-term dance partner as Astaire was, Kelly danced with many women on film, and his style was inspiring.

© Corbis

Gene Kelly, a major star of the Hollywood musical, had a casual style that many viewers could relate to.

I got started dancing because I knew it was one way to meet girls.

Gene Kelly

The Hollywood musical was a major force from the 1930s into the mid-1950s. Fred Astaire, Ginger Rogers, Gene Kelly, Eleanor Powell, Van Johnson, Donald O'Connor, Cyd Charisse, Ann Miller, and countless others brought partner dancing alive on film and made the viewer want to dance. Many of the dance films in the thirties and forties were film versions of stage musicals of the day. Some of the films included backstage settings and visits to a theater or nightclub built into the plot. Partner dances blossomed while they were featured on the big screen in their natural setting and also danced on stage as a show within the show. Another interesting aspect of the dances on film from the era is how the movement in many of them was inspired by or grew out of simply walking. Hermes Pan (Fred Astaire's main choreographer for many of his films) was a genius at that and showed how simple movement could turn into glorious dance. The musicals of the Great Depression (and indeed even the World War II years) allowed Americans to escape from economic reality into the glamorous fantasy world that Hollywood offered. While dancing, couples never worried about bank closings, falling stock prices, and overdue rent. They simply danced, fell in love, and lived happily ever after.

Another major force in American style ballroom dancing was Arthur Murray, and he truly made his mark during the thirties and forties. He started teaching dance in 1913 at a huge exhibition hall in New York City. Feeling he needed more lessons to become a better teacher himself, he studied under Vernon and Irene Castle. He eventually developed ballroom dance schools and trained teachers to teach the general public. Murray was a keen businessman. At a very young age he began a mail order business as a way to sell his dance lessons. After a false start using kinetoscopes, devices that show moving pictures, he moved on to drawing and selling footprints, which dancers could place on the floor to learn the dance steps. By the time he married Kathryn in 1925, his mail order dance business was netting him $35,000 a year, after only six years in business. He opened a dance studio at 11 E. 43rd Street in New York City that encompassed eight floors. Although the effects of the stock market crash reduced the studio to just two floors, the business thrived, and in 1938, the first officially franchised Arthur Murray dance studio opened in Minneapolis, Minnesota. The Arthur Murray name was further etched into the public eye in the 1942 film, *The Fleet's In*, in which Betty Hutton sang the Johnny Mercer tune (with the Jimmy Dorsey Orchestra) "Arthur Murray Taught Me Dancing in a Hurry." By 1946, there were 72 Arthur Murray Studios across the country, which grew into franchised schools all over the world.

Fred Astaire, arguably one of the greatest dancers of all time, was thought to be a natural dancer by many people. However, he knew the importance of good training. In fact, Mr. Astaire was quoted as saying, "Some people seem to think that good dancers are born, but all the good dancers I have known are taught or trained." In 1947, Fred Astaire was convinced by friend and film producer Charles Casanave to open a new dance studio on Park Avenue in New York City. It seemed like a natural idea. A March 17, 1947 *Time* magazine article titled "Dancing Feat" reported that the new studio would be quite plush, with "deep red carpets, blue-green walls, yellow and red covered furniture. There, at $70 for a ten-hour course, Astaire hopes to teach all comers to dance something like Astaire." Although Fred Astaire didn't actually teach, more than 80 instructors were hired and trained to pass along his prowess on the floor. There were requests for 75 franchises in the first year alone, and now there are Fred Astaire Dance Studios all over the world. In 1958, when

Mr. Casanave passed away, Mr. Astaire wanted to pursue other interests and sold his portion of the business to Charles Casanave's two sons.

When the United States entered World War II in 1941, all industry was geared toward the war effort. War production pulled the country out of the Great Depression. Unemployment essentially disappeared. Most men were drafted and sent off to war, so women and the black population were allowed to fill their jobs. Until that time, generally only unmarried women worked, but suddenly, out of necessity, married women joined the workforce. Many women found that they were as capable as men and were making decisions, running companies, and even building aircraft. South American and Latin dances, such as the samba, mambo, rumba, and cha cha, were making a big hit. With the men off to war, women were gaining confidence and independence, and the sensuous freedom of the dances was met with enthusiasm. Women were learning they could hold their own with men and enjoyed being out and about more. The jitterbug was in full force, and GIs took the dance overseas when they went to war. They taught the dance to local girls and barmaids and even danced with each other if necessary. Many of the singers with the big bands were striking out on their own. The stylings of Bing Crosby, Dinah Shore, Frank Sinatra, and Perry Como were becoming popular on the music charts. When the war ended and the GIs returned, the marriage rate exploded. In 1946, the first nonwar year, the marriage rate jumped by almost 50 percent, and the baby boom generation was begun. Between 1946 and 1961, birth rates skyrocketed. And now that resources were no longer funneled to the war effort, television, which had been introduced at the 1939 World's Fair in New York, was taking hold and would change American entertainment for good.

1950s: Birth of Rock 'n' Roll

The postwar years sparked a sharp increase in the economy. The job market was booming. People were feeling optimistic: building homes, buying cars, and raising families. The key word in 1950s America was *conservative*, in everything—in dress, politics, religion, and social activities. Traditional family roles seemed to be the way: Dad went to work, Mom took care of the house, and families sat down to dinner together and discussed their day. Social rules in the early 1950s were strict. Teenagers learned proper etiquette and how to ask for a dance and how to accept. Dance classes were taught at school, and schools held dances where parents dropped off and picked up their teenage sons and daughters. But if the first half of the fifties were a time of strict codes, the second half of the decade demonstrated the teenagers' need to rebel and seek excitement. By 1956, there were 13 million teenagers in the country, and they wanted to define themselves. The birth of rock 'n' roll allowed the new generation to make its mark. When Bill Haley and the Comets released their hit record "Rock Around the Clock" in 1955, the rock 'n' roll sound was born. Kids found what they were looking for in the new music. Elvis Presley burst onto the scene in the mid-1950s, and Americans were taken by his sound, dubbing him the King of Rock 'n' Roll and catapulting him to international stardom. Poodle skirts became the fashion for many reasons. They were easy to dance in because they allowed for more mobility, they left lots of room to swing and emphasize the movement, and they were a statement of freedom symbolized by the free movement of the skirt and petticoats. Even though rock 'n' roll was on the scene, the music seemed to peacefully coexist with the gentler sounds of Pat Boone, Connie Francis, Patti Page, Perry Como, Peggy Lee, and Bobby Darin. Although young people were experiencing more freedom and independence, they were still, on the whole, respectful to adults and their parents.

Television, on hold during the war years, was now making its real appearance. Movies, especially lavish Hollywood musicals, seemed to be on the decline as Americans bought this new invention and brought entertainment right into their living rooms. Radio programs were making the leap to television, and new styles of programs were being developed for the new medium. *The Ed Sullivan Show*, *I Love Lucy*, and *The Honeymooners* were in everyone's home. *Your Hit Parade*, a popular radio program that made a transfer to television, was a success in the first half of the decade, featuring the most popular songs of the previous week. But when rock 'n' roll entered the scene, the rather staid show lost its appeal with younger viewers and aired its last program in 1959. *American Bandstand*, however, fared much better. It influenced popular dance immensely and was a huge hit. It debuted on October 7, 1952, in Philadelphia as Bob Horn's *Bandstand*. In 1956, 26-year-old Dick Clark took over as host, and the show was picked up by ABC and renamed *American Bandstand*. Teenagers tuned in daily to see the latest dances. Group dances became quite popular in the 1950s. One of the most popular was the stroll, in which guys and girls formed two parallel lines. The lines of dancers did a basic step in unison, such as a side together touch. The guy and girl at one end of the line paired off and danced down the path created by the two lines, then parted and rejoined the end of their respective lines. Everyone moved up, and the next couple danced through, and so on. In a sense, the stroll was similar in basic form to some of the contra dances that had been around for centuries. Even though the music, steps, and style were updated, the basic process was the same: Lines of dancers performing the same steps. Other group dances and novelty dances, sometimes called party dances, introduced in the fifties were the Madison, the hand jive, the hokey pokey, and the bunny hop (then later the bunny hop mambo). Some of those dances endure today as mixers at many gatherings and dances. As a holdover from the thirties and forties, the swing (or jitterbug) continued to be popular. The 1950s are also considered to be the golden age of Cuban music, and Americans enjoyed import dances like the mambo and the cha cha. By the early sixties, however, the Cuban music and dances fell out of the mainstream because of two major events: the Communist revolution in Cuba and the British invasion of such bands as the Beatles.

The husband-and-wife dance team of Marge and Gower Champion was immensely popular, and they have been called the Vernon and Irene Castle of the 1950s. Their many film, television, and stage appearances won them the hearts of many fans of musicals and partner dancing. They had great style and personality, and achieved acclaim not only as dancers, but also as directors and choreographers for many hit musicals on stage and screen.

Arthur and Kathryn Murray hosted their television show, *The Arthur Murray Party*, which aired from 1950 to 1960. The popular social dances were performed by a group of Arthur Murray Dance Studio instructors, and the highlight of the show was a lesson segment with audience participation. That television show brought ballroom dancing into people's living rooms all over the country and enticed customers to the studios to learn how to dance. In a sense, their television program was not only entertainment but also an advertisement for their dance schools, and people flocked to learn not only the latest dances, such as the mambo and the cha cha, but also the classic dances, such as the foxtrot and the waltz.

Fred Astaire hosted his own variety special in 1958 called *An Evening With Fred Astaire*. It was so successful it was rebroadcast in 1959 and 1964. It was the first program to be rerun using color videotape. Because of the success of that program, Astaire went on to star in three similar specials: *Another Evening With Fred Astaire* (1959), *Astaire Time* (1960), and *The Fred Astaire Show* (1968). His partner on all of those specials was a beautiful and talented dancer named Barrie Chase.

Many of the popular dances of the late 1950s continued to enjoy their popularity into the early sixties. But the times were changing. The Federal Highway Act was signed, allowing work to begin on the interstate highway system, and passenger air travel was dawning, which would allow people to travel greater distances more easily. The Civil Rights movement began on December 1, 1955, when Rosa Parks refused to give up her bus seat to a white man. Conservatism and anticommunist feelings were prevalent, and McCarthyism was in full swing. The Vietnam War was imminent. The seemingly blissful utopia of the fifties was lending way to the turbulence of the sixties, and the music and dancing would be mirrored in those changes.

1960s: Rock 'n' Roll and Turbulent Times

The times, they were indeed a-changin'. The Vietnam War; the space program; the arrival of the Beatles; the assassinations of President John F. Kennedy, civil rights leaders Martin Luther King, Jr., and Robert Kennedy; and finally Woodstock were some of the major events of the decade. Skirts went from leftover 1950s bouffants in the early sixties, to shorter-than-short miniskirts in the middle of the decade, then finally down-to-the-floor maxiskirts when the hippie look came in at the end of the decade. It was an era of people trying to make a statement. Partner dancing didn't allow people the individual freedom to make their own statements, but the solo dances did. Even if danc-ing in front of a partner, they were still dancing alone in a sense. Alone, yet together. That seemed to be the message in the dancing, as well as in the life philosophy of the times.

During the 1960s, it seems there were new dances every week, almost mir-roring had happened in the first two decades of the 1900s (there were even new animal dances!). As a new song was released, there was almost surely a dance to go along with it. Chubby Checker's "The Twist" was perhaps the most famous, and the one with the most staying power. The twist was an especially easy dance to pick up, which certainly helped it spread quickly. One simply placed the ball of his or her foot over an imaginary dropped cigarette and twisted it back and forth, as if trying to extinguish it. At the same time, one held an imaginary bath towel and pulled it from side to side as if drying off one's behind. Simple, but with as much movement and energy as the individual dancer wanted to put into it. Other songs that had dances associated with them were "Pony Time" (the pony), "Mashed Potato Time" (the mashed potato), "The Loco-Motion" and the "Peppermint Twist." The appearance of solo dancing in the 1960s was perhaps a sign of the begin-nings of the sexual revolution; women finally broke free of men's control in couple dancing.

American Bandstand was still going strong on television. But other programs on television in the sixties also featured young people doing the dances of the day. *Hullabaloo*, introduced in 1965, featured a team of four men and six women demonstrating the latest dances. And unlike *American Bandstand*, which began as a daily telecast but for most of its run aired on Saturday afternoons, *Hullabaloo* aired during prime time. Both shows featured the top songs of the day, with many live appearances by the artists. Other similar TV programs of the sixties included *The Buddy Deane Show*, *The Clay Cole Show*, and *The Milt Grant Show* (actually begun in the late fifties).

Go-go dancers in miniskirts and knee-high go-go boots danced in elevated cages. One of the first clubs to feature go-go dancers was the Whisky a Go Go in West Hollywood, California. The Whisky a Go Go has been considered the first American discotheque, a club playing only recordings, employing no live bands. Before she became known as a serious actress, Goldie Hawn brought the image of the go-go dancer into people's homes on the television series *Rowan & Martin's Laugh-In*.

Dance was not an important aspect of the late 1960s, mostly because of the undanceable nature of the music. The hippie generation was upon us, and the music that was in vogue was folk rock and what has been referred to as psychedelic. Long instrumental solos with many electronic effects were featured in the music played by bands like Pink Floyd, the Doors, Jefferson Airplane, and Grateful Dead. The music wasn't so much for dancing to, but listening to. That would continue into the early seventies when touch dancing would make a comeback.

Although traditional partner dancing was not in the mainstream during that time, there were still devotees of the dances of the past. Dance studios continued to teach them, and a niche market still existed. The teenagers and young adults were still rebelling, but their parents, who grew up with the foxtrot, waltz, tango, and other more traditional partner dances, continued to enjoy them. But they were considered old-fashioned by the newer, hip generation.

1970s: Disco Reigns Supreme

In 1976, novelist Tom Wolfe coined the expression the "Me Decade" to define the 1970s. And he was essentially accurate. After the social activism of the 1960s, the 1970s saw a shift in consciousness to social activities for one's own pleasure. People proudly had an analyst (or a guru of some sort) and joined therapy groups. Drug use became rampant, and the sexual revolution was in full swing, with the divorce rate and premarital sex both on the rise. The music that made an emergence mid-decade clearly exemplified the shift toward hedonism. Many people remember the 1970s with one word: disco. And for good reason. Although a relatively short-lived style, disco music and disco dancing had an enormous impact on the evolution of dancing and dance music that is felt to the present day. Disco music was centered on an electronic drumbeat and synthesizers and was often repetitive and mesmerizing. The steady disco beat felt like blood pumping through one's veins, and people flocked to the dance floor to move to the new sound. In 1975, Van McCoy's song "The Hustle" started a dance craze with a line dance by the same name. By the time the movie *Saturday Night Fever* was released in 1977, the hustle (which became a catchall phrase for many of the disco dances of the decade) was huge. In *Saturday Night Fever*, John Travolta played a New York City youth who goes to a local disco on the weekends. There, he is the king of the dance floor and is able to forget the reality of his troubled life. The music of the Bee Gees was featured in the film, which helped the soundtrack to become a huge hit on the charts around the world. A few of the multitudes of musical artists of the day who figured heavily in the disco phenomenon include Donna Summer, the Village People, Gloria Gaynor, and ABBA.

Saturday Night Fever was one of the most instrumental films in creating an influx of people running to dance studios to learn to dance. After more than a decade of people not touching each other while dancing, here was a new style that people saw on the big screen creating romance and sensuality, and they wanted to learn to do it too. Dance studios were eager to teach the hustle and then introduce the new dance students to other dances. That was not too difficult because the hustle had roots in swing and cha cha and several other partner dances. Dance teachers explained that learning the other dances would enhance their understanding of the hustle. The hustle spawned many versions of itself, including the tango hustle and the Latin hustle.

Shortly after the release of *Saturday Night Fever, Thank God It's Friday* (another disco-themed film) was released in 1978. Dancing was again highly visible on television as well. *American Bandstand*, still going strong and always featuring the current music and dances, brought disco into everyone's living room. Don Cornelius hosted *Soul Train*, debuting in the early seventies and featuring primarily African American dancers and recording artists. Merv Griffin produced *Dance Fever*, hosted by Deney Terrio and later Adrian Zmed. On that television program, three celebrities judged dancers while they performed to the biggest disco hits of the day.

© Corbis

People flocked to Studio 54 during the disco craze to be seen near celebrities such as Liza Minnelli and Mikhail Baryshnikov, shown here demonstrating the flashy dance style of the late 1970s.

The strobe lighting and mirror balls in the discos inspired a sense of fashion that included stretchy, sequined bandeau tops for women and colorful polyester shirts unbuttoned to reveal men's chests sporting a gold chain or two. Gold lamé, spandex, and anything with sequins that caught the light and showed off the body were necessary for being fashionably dressed when going out to dance. Platform shoes were a must for both sexes. Discotheques in large metropolitan cities became exclusive nightclubs, where doormen were selective in whom they admitted behind the red velvet ropes. Studio 54, which opened in 1977, was one the most sought-after places to be seen during the disco era. Stylishly dressed "nobodies" waited outside hoping to gain entry so they could be seen near and dance next to celebrities in the chic club on West 54th Street in New York City. Discos were packing in crowds all over the country. One of the biggest effects disco had was inspiring the resurgence of touch dancing, dancing *with* a partner, not merely *in front of* one. Sensuality was back in style and so was partner dancing. In 1979, David Naughton starred in a television sitcom version of *Saturday Night Fever* called *Makin' It*, but the series didn't even make it through an entire season. Disco was on the way out.

1980s: A Return to Elegance and Conservatism

In the latter-1960s and throughout the seventies, permissiveness permeated society. But the sexual revolution had taken its toll. With the onset of AIDS in the early eighties and other sexually transmitted diseases on the rise, people now wanted to take their time to get to know one another. A slower romantic style was suddenly in vogue again, and ballroom dancing would once again prove to be a vehicle for that. The buzzword in the United States in the 1980s was *conservatism*—both socially and politically. Ronald Reagan was the president for most of the decade, and he and his wife, Nancy, brought a conservative view to America. They were a refined couple, and they gave elegance to the White House. Because Ronald and Nancy Reagan had been film actors, they were accustomed to the glamorous Hollywood style. The Reagans entertained in the White House with style, and consequently, black-tie affairs and ballrooms again were in vogue. The 1980s were a time of conspicuous consumption, and ballroom dancing was a perfect outlet for affluent society to dress up and spend money.

The disco days of the seventies waged into the early eighties, but many more types of music were waiting on the horizon. Country and western, punk, hip-hop, rap, and new wave (a sort of fusion of pop, rock, and disco) were all making appearances in the eighties. It was an extremely diverse decade for music, which of course made the dancing just as eclectic. The two artists who probably made the biggest impression on music in the eighties were Michael Jackson and Madonna. Cable television was born, and MTV (Music Television) was launched in 1981. Madonna and Michael Jackson used this new venue to the fullest, creating music videos with elaborate dance sequences. In 1983, CMT (Country Music Television) was invited into American homes, and in 1985 VH1 (Video Hits One) joined the TV music frenzy. Music videos had an immense influence on the younger generation, not just in music and dance, but also in pop culture. Olivia Newton-John's hit song and music video "Let's Get Physical" came along in 1982 when the fitness craze in the United States was dawning. Jane Fonda and Richard Simmons inspired people to work out with their best-selling videos. As a result, people flocked to gyms, aerobics studios, and dance studios to get in shape.

Dancing was featured in several feature films of the eighties, such as *Staying Alive*, the 1983 sequel to *Saturday Night Fever*, again starring John Travolta. *Urban Cowboy*, another Travolta film released in 1980, brought country and western dancing to the public in a big way. What had been a niche style suddenly became a major dance trend in America. Ballroom studios began to offer classes in the two-step (danced by John Travolta and Debra Winger in *Urban Cowboy*) and other country and western dances. Although still widely danced in many circles, the big country and western trend lasted roughly from the early eighties through the early nineties.

Fashion trends also were inspired by the films of the decade. Professional dance wear, such as leggings and legwarmers, became fashionable street wear, partly because of the movie *Flashdance*, released in 1983. The movie *Fame*, and subsequent television series, contributed to that trend as well. Other dance movies of the decade included *Footloose* in 1984, which was set in a small town where rock music and dancing had been banned by local government. And then there was the immensely popular hit movie *Dirty Dancing*. In that 1987 film (set in 1963), a young girl falls in love with a dance instructor at a Catskills resort. Patrick Swayze and Jennifer Grey had a chemistry that made the dancing all that much more exciting, and the romantic and sensual energy inspired more people to dance.

It was in the 1980s that ballroom dancing as a performance art was brought to a wider audience, an audience that didn't necessarily dance but did enjoy watching dance as a spectator event. Ballroom dance companies emerged and took the art and style of ballroom dancing to the stage. Two of the most well-known companies were American Ballroom Theater and Peter Maxwell's Ballroom Dance Theater, both headed by internationally acclaimed ballroom dancers. In those companies, talented and respected dancers from the ballroom world combined the romance and style of ballroom dancing with the excitement of live theater to create magic. Several ballroom dancers also appeared on Broadway stages, including American and Canadian champion Victoria Regan, who appeared in the original Broadway company of *42nd Street* (directed and choreographed by Gower Champion). Pierre Dulaine and Yvonne Marceau, world champions and founders of American Ballroom Theater, took their inimitable style to Broadway in the 1989 production of *Grand Hotel*. With the public enjoying the theatricality of partner dancing again, the tango was the star in the 1985 Broadway production *Tango Argentino* and in the 1988 film *Tango Bar*. Tango became a popular dance once again, and dance studios were thrilled with the influx of people wanting to learn it.

In 1980, the television station WGBH in Boston and hundreds of PBS affiliates began to broadcast the United States Ballroom Championships and then later one of the biggest dance competitions in the United States, the Ohio Star Ball. What started out as a one-time special presentation turned out to be a huge hit, and it became a yearly special. Rita Moreno was the host of that first special, and subsequent PBS hosts included Juliet Prowse, Sandy Duncan, Barbara Eden, Marilu Henner, and Jasmine Guy. The show, called *Championship Ballroom Dancing* (and a later version called *America's Ballroom Challenge*), brought competition dancing into people's homes in the same way that *The Arthur Murray Party* took social dancing to the public.

1990s and Beyond: Here to Stay

The changing face of ballroom dance is evident today in many ways. The resurgence that ballroom dancing experienced in the 1980s continued into the 1990s. The media, always persuasive, continued to be influential. Movies, commercials, television sitcoms, and even reality shows have included partner dancing in their plots. A plethora of films released in the 1990s and into the twenty-first century have shown ballroom dancing either in a social situation or at a competitive level. In the 1992 film *Scent of a Woman*, Al Pacino danced a tango. The 2005 documentary *Mad Hot Ballroom* detailed the ballroom dance program for elementary school children in New York City public schools, Dancing Classrooms, launched by Pierre Dulaine and Yvonne Marceau. In 2006, Antonio Banderas starred in *Take the Lead*, a fictional film based on Dancing Classrooms. Films featuring a plot about competition ballroom dancing include *Strictly Ballroom* (1992), *Dance With Me* (1998) with Vanessa L. Williams, and the Japanese film *Shall We Dansu?* (1996). Released in 1997 in the United States with English subtitles, *Shall We Dansu?* was so popular that it was remade as *Shall We Dance?* in English in 2004 with stars Richard Gere, Jennifer Lopez, and Susan Sarandon. Other films that included ballroom dancing were *Tango* (1998), *Dirty Dancing: Havana Nights* (2004), and *Marilyn Hotchkiss' Ballroom Dancing and Charm School* (2005). The popular sitcoms *Will & Grace* (1998-2006) and *Friends* (1994-2004) had episodes that mentioned ballroom dancing competitions, and the stars even did a little dancing of their own. Reality TV brought ballroom dancing into America's living rooms on a greater level than ever before. *Ballroom Bootcamp* took ordinary people through a vigorous five-week training program, and then set them loose on the floor at a competition. *So You Think You Can Dance* features trained dancers from a variety of styles—ballroom, ballet, contemporary, hip-hop—and partners them to compete against each other every week in a different style. On *Dancing With the Stars*, celebrities are partnered with highly ranked dancers from the ballroom world. Each week, the soap opera stars, talk show hosts, newscasters, singers, and big-name athletes compete against each other in a new dance. Commercials got into the ballroom act as well. The Gap featured swing dancing on television commercials in 1998. All of the exposure in film and on television helped to create a renewed interest in ballroom dancing and generated more business for dance studios.

As ballroom dancing made it into the younger generation's films and television programs, it became a hit with the college crowd. It had always been taught in some fashion on some college campuses (such as Brigham Young University, which continues to turn out some of the best young ballroom competitors in the country), but then the word started spreading. Ballroom dancing became cool! It was the thing to do, and it seemed that almost every college offered some sort of dancing and even assembled teams of dancers to go to competitions. With organizations like USA Dance and local dance studios behind them, college kids learned from the best and helped ballroom dancing become even bigger.

Ballroom dancing was definitely sweeping the nation, so a National Ballroom Dance Week seemed appropriate. In 1989, a Ballroom Week was promoted in New York City by Mary Helen McSweeney. The event was such a success and drew so much publicity, that in 1990 the editors of several of the major ballroom publications got together and proposed a National Ballroom

Dance Week, and the idea took off. It was held in September of 1990, and every September since. In 1991, it was extended to 10 days in order to have two anchor weekends for even more dancing events. The purpose of National Ballroom Dance Week is to spread the word about ballroom dancing to a larger public, to demonstrate the benefits of dancing, and to promote the industry as a whole. During National Ballroom Dance Week, dance studios and dance clubs host free dance lessons and demonstrations. Businesses (and even government organizations) donate space for promotions and public demonstrations of dance. Exhibitions, dance shows, and dance lessons are held in senior homes, hospitals, hospices, schools, colleges, and shopping malls across the country.

It seems that as new music and dances have emerged, the younger generation has always latched on and dismissed the previously established styles as old-fashioned. As we have seen, this has been happening for centuries. But being retro makes a comeback periodically, so the dances of yesterday return to fashion. The media, greatly influencing the trends and styles of every generation, are also responsive to the public's needs and desires, and are quick to follow suit. Culture, society, music, and fashion all change, but there will always be people of various ages attracted to dancing with a partner. Moving to music and dancing with a partner have been popular for centuries and will remain a huge part of the culture of each particular era. The joy of dancing together has been on the upswing for decades, and it shows no sign of slowing. Ballroom dancing is here to stay, and it seems that what one used to think of as something your grandparents did is not old-fashioned at all. Around the world, children are taught ballroom dancing almost as soon as they can walk. They grow up with it. That idea is taking root in the United States now as well, and as the younger generations grow up with ballroom dancing from an early age, they will carry it on through their lives: children taking their first steps and learning to foxtrot, college kids learning the tango and going to competitions between studying for exams, adults celebrating events with a waltz, and grandparents dancing a Viennese waltz and reminiscing. It's for every generation, and people of every age will continue to enjoy the benefits and joy of ballroom dancing.

Dancing as a Hobby

Why are people captivated by ballroom dancing? Is it the old-fashioned ballroom, the beautiful gowns, the soft lights, a big band, and two people gliding effortlessly across the floor? Is it the romance? If you're reading this book, you already have some interest in learning to dance. But why? What brought you to this decision? Most people have a definite reason for wanting to learn to dance: to dance at a relative's wedding, to meet new people, or to exercise. People who grew up without partner dancing may gravitate toward dancing with a partner because of the intimacy and contact it provides in contrast to what they have been used to doing. For instance, those solitary dancers from the 1960s who didn't experience touch dancing may seek something they believe they have missed out on. But even people who grew up with partner dancing may be nostalgic to return to that earlier time. People who enjoyed the Lindy of the 1940s or even the hustle in the 1970s and 1980s may want to rekindle that excitement.

Understanding your motives for learning to dance will make the process more enjoyable and will accelerate your learning. If you understand what you want to accomplish by dancing, you can structure your learning and practice time to achieve those goals. For instance, if you are learning to dance for exercise, you will certainly want to dance more than a few minutes per week. And if you're learning to dance so you can meet new people, you will need to take the dancing out of your living room at some point and into a more public dance venue.

Dancing means different things to different people, and people learn to dance to fulfill many needs. Most people agree that dancing is physical movement done to sounds. But is dancing an art, a sport, or a social activity? Or is it a combination of the three? This chapter explores the various views of dancing and the physical, mental, emotional, and social benefits of learning to dance as a hobby.

DANCING AS ART

Let's begin by defining what we mean by art. Purely speaking, it's the human effort to imitate, supplement, alter, or counteract the work of nature. Well, that certainly encompasses a multitude of things in seemingly endless combinations. And after we determine whether or not something is indeed art, there is the question of whether it is good art or bad art. But then it becomes even *more* subjective. It can be safely assumed that art can be many things to many people. So, then, the creator, observer, or participant can define art as he or she wants to. American poet Amy Lowell said, "Art is the desire of a man to express himself, to record the reactions of his personality to the world he lives in." Self-expression, then, is art, and dance can fulfill that criterion.

For people who consider dancing an art, the combination of the music and movement brings beauty into their lives. They see the beauty and elegance of the two bodies moving together as one. They most enjoy the feelings they have as they glide across the floor in a smooth dance or the rhythmic sensations in Latin music. Dancing also provides an artistic outlet for people to express themselves. In Volume III, Issue 6 of *Dance Notes*, Shalene Archer Ermis, former United States professional ballroom champion, said, "What separates us from the other sports is movement to music. It has to come more from the heart than who crosses the finish line first." And for many people, the music is truly what makes it an artistic venture, even while training and competing like world-class athletes. Feeling the music, allowing it to move through the body and seeing what images it conjures, then expressing those emotions through movement can be a beautiful experience, and truly an artful one. In the same issue of *Dance Notes*, many other dancers expressed their views. World-class dancesport adjudicator Taliat Tarsinov said, "Dance is emotionally based and expresses the feelings within the human soul." Professional international standard competitor Vitaliy Logishev concurred, saying, "Dancing is communication and expression between two people."

Many people with analytical tendencies dance to help balance those tendencies with their artistic side. People who work primarily with the left side of the brain (such as engineers and other people with analytical occupations) may explore dancing as art to realize the processes of the right side of the brain, which governs more artistic and abstract thought. Not that dancing can't be technical and analytical—quite the contrary. To become a good dancer, a fair amount of technical learning must take place. That technical side may be what draws analytical people to dancing, but often they are pleased to discover a side of themselves they had never experienced: the artistic side.

> It's expression. Unfortunately it's not like a painting you can hang on the wall and save forever. Our canvas disappears after those two minutes.
>
> *Corky Ballas, world Latin finalist,* Dance Notes, *Vol. IV, Issue 3*

Even watching others dance can be an artistic experience. The opening sentence in Kenneth Laws' 2002 book, *Physics and the Art of Dance: Understanding Movement* reads: "Dance is an art form intended to communicate images that appeal to the aesthetic sensibilities of observers." From the earliest days of partner dancing, in addition to actively participating, people enjoyed *watching* others dance. As we observed in chapter 1, the court dances were done both socially and as performances. Since then, we have continued to be entertained by watching dancers create beautiful movement. From Vernon and Irene Castle performing their Castle walk, to Fred Astaire and Ginger Rogers gliding across the silver screen, to Patrick Swayze and Jennifer Grey discovering romance through dance in *Dirty Dancing*, we are captivated by the art of movement known as dance. When those couples performed, they were not merely executing a series of calculated dance steps, but they were also conveying emotion—a sense of something that other artists may express through painting, sculpture, singing, or any art form. But those artists used dance as their medium. As we discovered in chapter 1, ballroom dance companies formed in the 1980s took ballroom dancing to the stage to be viewed in much the same way one might view a ballet performance. Broadway shows have featured ballroom dancing, ballroom dancers have been featured on television programs and in films, and a hit stage show called *Burn the Floor* played in sold-out sports arenas around the world and ushered a new wave of ballroom dancing as performance art on a grand scale into the twenty-first century. Whether sitting in the audience of an elaborate show watching many couples create a ballroom extravaganza on a huge stage or simply sitting at a table at a small intimate dinner dance and watching an elegant couple whirl by dancing a beautiful waltz, you are appreciating dance as art.

There are several venues in which to express dance as art. Many dance studios hold showcases, where dancers perform a choreographed routine. Those are usually not judged events, so the performance is for the sake of performance, not winning. In preparing for a performance in a showcase, the dancer has a definite goal in mind. The dance must be choreographed, learned, and perfected by the performance date, so it's very much like rehearsing for a show. Showcases are helpful because the dancer also watches performances by his or her peers. A lot can be gained from this: seeing other styles or techniques that the dancer may want to learn, getting feedback from peers on progress, or simply enjoying someone else's artistic expression. Dancing for art does not have to be a public performance, however. Simply dancing at a social event may allow people to make an artistic statement, either to themselves, to their partners, or to the people who happen to see them dancing by. Two of the ideas discussed in the quotes at the beginning of this section are *self-expression* and *communication*. Connecting with another human being through music and movement is art. Really listen to the music, let it touch you deeply, and see what happens. Allow yourself to enjoy the artistry of a graceful waltz or foxtrot around the floor.

DANCING AS SPORT

We defined art, so now let's define sport: physical activity that is governed by a set of rules or customs and often engaged in competitively. Ballroom dancing fulfills that need as well. Ballroom dancing is indeed a physical activity, and when it is danced at a competition, one must follow certain rules. The major governing bodies of those competitions in the United States are the National Dance Council of America (NDCA) and USA Dance (formerly United States Amateur Ballroom Dancers Association).

Whether a person is dancing in a competition or not, ballroom dancing is still a sportlike activity. Participants who think dancing is a sport usually dance for the exercise and physical benefits it gives them. Dancing provides many health benefits. It is a great aerobic activity, works the cardiovascular system, and increases lung capacity. It balances cholesterol and levels of blood sugar in the body. Dancing improves posture and balance and quickens reflexes.

Dancing also burns calories. According to the Web site www.calorie-count.com, a 150-pound (68-kilogram) person will burn 204 calories per hour while dancing a slow waltz or foxtrot. But doing a faster dance (such as the cha cha or swing), a 150-pound person will burn 374 calories per hour. The Web site for NutriStrategy nutrition and fitness software (www.nutristrategy.com) lists similar findings: a 155-pound (70-kilogram) person burns 211 calories per hour during slower ballroom dancing, while faster ballroom dancing burns 387 calories per hour. Depending on the duration, speed, and intensity of the dancing, the calories burned can be significant. According to an article in the *Dancescape* e-zine titled "The Benefits of Dancing" (www.dancescape.com/ezine/healthbody/2004071901_benefits.htm), the muscle exertion and breathing rates of competitive ballroom dancers are comparable to athletes competing in cycling, swimming, and track events.

Ballroom dancing can provide quite a workout. Professional athletes are seeing the virtues of ballroom dancing as a sport. Retired NFL wide receiver Jerry Rice appeared on the second season of the television program *Dancing With the Stars*, finishing the competition in second place. In a July 2, 2006 *Parade* magazine article titled "Kick up your Heels," he told author Michael O'Shea, "I lost 14 pounds during those eight weeks of dancing—and, at 212 pounds, I was in good shape to begin with. But I liked the way my body changed. I stayed strong yet became leaner, more flexible and fluid." Wishing he had danced while he was still playing professional football, Mr. Rice said, "That added flexibility and awareness of my body would have helped prevent injuries."

> **F**ive hours of practice is sport. Stamina training and stretches are sport. What I create on the floor is art.
>
> *Louis van Amstel, world Latin champion*, Dance Notes, Vol. III, Issue 6

Many people do not exercise because they have the perception that most forms of exercise are too difficult or boring, but ballroom dancing can be a way to get healthier and have fun at the same time. The exercise and health benefits become almost a side effect of an enjoyable activity. In "You should be dancing, for the rhythm of your heart," a September 3, 2006 press release from the World Congress of Cardiology, Dr. Hermes Ilarraza of the National Institute of Cardiology in Mexico City stated that "dancing can improve physical capacity in heart patients much like other traditional training modalities, such as indoor cycling or aerobics. Ballroom dancing has the added benefits of being fun and social. It is an attractive option for many and provides a good incentive to exercise." Phil Martin, a kinesiology and physical education professor at California State University at Long Beach who has studied the effects of dance as exercise for more than 17 years, was quoted in the Fall 2006 edition of the university's magazine, *The Beach Review*: "It is possible for dancers to burn calories at a faster rate than someone running a five-minute mile. The great thing about dancing is that even a few minutes of it combined with good music and socialization can improve your mood and your health." So, even dancing at a dinner dance can offer health benefits.

Learning to dance also helps brain function because dancers have to think about what they're doing and physically do it with a partner at the same time. A study on ballroom dancing and its effects on dementia and Alzheimer's disease was conducted by Dr. Joe Verghese and colleagues at Albert Einstein College of Medicine in the Bronx, New York. Their results were published in a June 19, 2003 article in *The New England Journal of Medicine* titled "Leisure Activities and the Risk of Dementia in the Elderly." They studied a group of 469 men and women from 1980 to 2001. Participants kept track of how frequently they performed certain hobbies. No significant association was found between performing physical activities and the risk of dementia, except for those who participated in ballroom dancing. People who frequently participated in ballroom dancing reduced their risk of dementia by 76 percent. These findings show that learning to partner dance is a demanding exercise both physically and mentally and can have positive effects on both physical and mental health.

Serious dancers believe that at a competitive level, ballroom dancing is physically demanding and should be recognized as a sport. Moreover, they think that inclusion in the Olympic Games will further solidify the legitimacy of its sport status. In the 1980s, the term *dancesport* started to be bandied about when referring to competition-style ballroom dancing. In 1990, the International Council of Amateur Dancers (ICAD), formed in 1957, changed its name to the International DanceSport Federation (IDSF). In large part because of the name change and the IDSF's push to gain worldwide recognition of dance as sport, the International Olympic Committee granted member status to the IDSF on September 8, 1997. That did not make dancesport an Olympic medal event; it simply set the ball in motion. However, dancesport did make an appearance as part of a huge demonstration in the closing ceremonies of the 2000 Sydney Olympic Games, using nearly 500 couples! But several sports commentators did not take it seriously. American commentator Bob Costas of NBC made a joke about Rita Moreno pulling a hamstring. Australian sportswriter Ray Chesterton wrote in *The Daily Telegraph*, "No man wearing a dinner suit and a haughty look should ever be in contention for an Olympic gold medal. A headwaiter's job maybe. But never an Olympic final. Dancing isn't sport. It's fast walking to music. How difficult can it be?"

The debate continues. The major rifts seem to be the distinction between art and sport and the subjective system of judging. Proponents argue that because ice dancing is a sport, why not dancesport? Critics cite that ice dancing is more difficult because it's done on ice. Many people have the perception of ballroom dancing as something that older people do to pass the time. But the athleticism of dancesport can't be denied. Thanks in large part to media coverage, the image of dancesport is changing. What is important to realize is that ballroom dancing can be a recreational activity, and dancesport can be a highly competitive athletic activity; they can coexist. Olympic inclusion seems promising, but dancesport will have to make appearances at other world sporting events first, such as the Pan American Games.

When we think of ballroom dancing for sport, two categories come into play: dancing for physical fitness and dancing for competition, or dancesport. They can occur simultaneously, of course. Showcases were mentioned earlier in the discussion of dance as art. Taking a showcase one step further, dance studios hold similar events that are adjudicated. The dancers may be judged against a standard or level of learning and receive a score. In that case, they are essentially competing against themselves, not other dancers. Or, they may be judged head to head with the other dancers and assigned a placement against them. On a larger scale, there is at least one dancesport event held every weekend somewhere in the country. For more information on how to get involved in competition dancing, refer to chapter 11. But one does not have to compete or perform to achieve the physical fitness that dancing can bring. Dancing at a social event once, twice, or five times a week (depending on your stamina) can bring wonderful physical benefits. But remember, if physical fitness is your goal, just going to the dance and chatting with your friends isn't enough; you need to dance!

DANCING AS SOCIAL ACTIVITY

Whether dancing for art or sport, most people who enter the world of ballroom dance begin for social reasons. Those reasons may evolve to include dancing for sport (such as competition dancing) or for art (such as exhibition performance dancing). But many dancers may not go those routes. They are content to enjoy all the benefits that can be garnered from social dancing.

Some people learn to dance for a specific social activity. Perhaps a wedding is coming up and they want to be able to get up and dance a few steps. Perhaps it's their daughter's wedding, and they will have to dance in front of people. Perhaps it's their own wedding, and all eyes will be on them for their first dance. Fear can be an incredible motivation to learn. If it's not a wedding, perhaps it's a class reunion, an office holiday party, or a formal event. Any of those events may feature a live band or orchestra or prerecorded music. A variety of music may be played, covering many styles of dance. The motivation for a man to learn to dance for one of those events may be to feel comfortable asking anyone to dance and be confident that he can lead his partner easily and without tripping her. For a woman, the motivation may be to feel confident that if asked to dance at an event, she can accept without embarrassment and follow any partner who asks her to dance. Or, if already partnered, perhaps the couple wants to be able to dance together simply for enjoyment. One thing to keep in mind is that if learning for a specific event, don't wait until a week or two before the event to start learning. It takes time to get comfortable, so give yourself as much time as you can to learn the different dances and steps so that you can truly enjoy the event. If your company has an office party every December, don't wait until November to start learning. If your wedding is in June, start planning and learning your dance in January. There is a lot of stress in the weeks preceding a wedding and many last-minute things to do, so allow for that so you can shine on your big day.

Many people dance for self-fulfillment or as a hobby. To them, dancing is for entertainment and for creating a social life. It's the opportunity to do something physical and at the same time enjoyable that's possibly very differ-

© Getty Images

Social dancing, whether for a specific event or a personal hobby, affords people of all skill levels a chance to interact with others who share a common interest.

ent from their daily work routine. If people sit at a desk all day in a cubicle, the need to be with other people and move around can be fulfilled through social dancing. Or if their daily work routine involves flying a plane, driving a cab, delivering mail, or serving restaurant patrons, ballroom dancing affords those people an opportunity to interact socially with others who share a common interest. It brings people together who may come from different walks of life but who share the joy of dance. Being at a social dance is a great way for people from different cultures and social backgrounds to get together and share the same dance interest. They dance to meet new people and form friendships.

Getting dressed up to go out dancing encourages people to be at their best. It helps them gain confidence in themselves. If you feel that you look good, you tend to feel better about yourself and consequently about your life. When getting ready to go out into a social situation where there might be dancing, people tend to spruce themselves up a bit with a nicely pressed outfit, well-coifed hair, and a splash of cologne. It's part of the ritual of going out. And when we know we are going to be in close contact with others, we may take even extra care to bring out our best.

Some people dance for romantic purposes. They want to enjoy an evening of dancing with their spouse or significant other. Or if single, they want to find a romantic partner. Through the ages, social dances have allowed people to mingle and perhaps partner up for more than a dance or two: for an evening, a few weeks or months, or even for a lifetime. The famous Roseland Ballroom, which opened in 1919 in New York City, has a plaque in the entrance listing hundreds of couples who met there and eventually married. And it started from dancing. When people share a common interest, they tend to gravitate toward one another. And if that common interest includes physical touch, such as in a dance position, and beautiful romantic music is playing, it can open the door to romance.

Many dancers who dance competitively still recognize, and indeed appreciate, the social aspects of ballroom dancing. In Volume III, Issue 6 of *Dance Notes*, world champion ballroom dancer Pierre Dulaine said, "I don't really think dancing is a sport. I think it's social. People started learning dancing as a hobby." And in the same issue of *Dance Notes*, Jerry Freiberg, an amateur competitor, said, "I still think of dancing as fundamentally recreational, something you go out and do at night and have fun when you're not competing against anyone." Those dancers, and so many more, can differentiate what they do on the competition floor from what they do on the social dance floor. The social aspects of dancing are a part of human nature. In his 2007 book *Dance To Live*, John P. Lenhart, M.D., wrote, "Society has functioned in groups since the beginning of time. Thousands of years ago people were gathering together and dancing. Dancing has always been a means by which people could get together and have a wonderful time."

Venues for social dancing are numerous. Many dance studios hold open dance parties. Amateur dance organizations, such as USA Dance, hold dances across the country. Nightclubs, cruises, weddings, society events, and even backyard barbecues may offer the opportunity to dance the night away. Dance parties at studios and through organizations often have mixers. These are especially advantageous for dancers who have come to the dance without a partner. There are various types of mixers, but they all serve more or less the same purpose. During the course of several songs, or often during one song, a dancer may have several different partners. This gives everyone a chance to dance with a variety of partners, some that you may not have thought of asking to dance. You may find an enjoyable partner that you had not danced with previously and will seek him or her out again.

> I think the whole dance world is about creating dreams that you want. Whether it is students, or professionals or amateurs, it's about trying to fulfill your dreams. When we dance, we learn so much about ourselves.
>
> *Paul Killick, world Latin finalist,* Dance Notes, *Vol. VI, Issue 1*

A topic that merits discussion is dancing with a disability. There is no reason this can't be done. People with missing limbs, who are deaf, who are blind, or who use wheelchairs dance. A prime example is Heather Mills, a social activist and former model who was hit by a motorcycle in 1993. A metal plate was put into her pelvis, and her left leg was amputated below the knee. In 2007 she danced on the television program *Dancing With the Stars*, making it through several rounds. Many people claimed that there was no way to tell that she had a disability. Dance courses all over the world allow people who use wheelchairs to ballroom dance. Some even dance at competitions. So, dancing really is for everyone.

In social dancing, the goal is enjoyment. There are no judges, no scorekeepers, and no rehearsals—just you, your partner, and the music. What more do you need? Enjoy the music, enjoy your partner, and dance the night away.

3

Connecting Music and Dance

Moving to the music is an integral part of dancing. The dances and the music are interconnected. Each dance was designed to express the music that is playing. In chapter 1, we looked at the history of ballroom dancing. Throughout history, as different styles of music emerged, the dances changed to reflect the type of music being played. To understand how to dance to the music, you need to understand what the music is telling you. Each of the rhythms conveys a feeling. The feelings can be romantic, energetic, fun, sexy, and many others, sometimes all in the same piece of music. To adequately express the music, you cannot dance the same dance to all music. The music determines the dance and creates the mood and movement of that particular dance. Because music is an integral part of dancing, understanding the music is an important factor in the learning process. This chapter will help you recognize the types of music that go along with the dances portrayed in this book: waltz, tango, foxtrot, and Viennese waltz. You will also learn how to find the beat in the music and how to use the beats to create a dance.

FINDING THE BEAT

Everything in life flows with a rhythm: a basketball being dribbled, the traffic on a highway, even the most basic activities in our lives, like brushing our teeth. Your heartbeat has a rhythm. Your breathing has a rhythm. When you walk, your footsteps have a rhythm. You may not be conscious of the rhythms in your daily life, but they are everywhere. Even though some people *think* that they have no rhythm, everyone has the ability to have rhythm when dancing. The challenge is to find that rhythm and match it to the rhythm of the music being played. Rhythm is the placement of sounds in time. In its most general sense, rhythm is an ordered alternation of contrasting elements. So music rhythm is a consistent pattern that makes the music flow.

> See this technique demonstrated on the DVD

But how do you find the specific rhythm of each song, and how do you match that rhythm to each dance? Some people hear it or feel it inherently. Some people need to work at it a little more. To better understand specific rhythms, especially those that may be new to you, let's explain a little bit about how music is written—in essence, what elements go into making a song that you can dance to. Although you will never have to read a piece of sheet music to dance, some people benefit from seeing the technical aspects of the written music.

Music is written on a staff, which consists of five horizontal parallel lines across a page. In writing music, several things are written at the beginning of the piece of music on the staff that provide basic information to the musicians playing the song. The only element we will concern ourselves with and the only one that has a direct impact on how to dance to the music is called the time signature. A time signature looks like a fraction, such as 2/4, 3/4, 4/4. The bottom number signifies what kind of note gets one count, or beat (the 4 means a quarter note gets one beat), and the top number tells us how many beats are in each measure. In dancing, the most important number in the time signature is the top number because it dictates how to count the music. Music is divided into measures (sometimes called bars), and a vertical line separates the measures. Only so many beats fit into each measure, which depends on the time signature. For example, in 4/4 time, only 4 counts may be placed in a measure. After that, a new measure must begin. Sometimes, there is no sound on a beat. This is called a rest, but it still counts as a beat. The dances taught in this book have only two time signatures. Foxtrot and tango music are written in 4/4 time, so that means there are four beats in a measure of music. Waltz and Viennese waltz are written in 3/4 time, so there are only three beats in a measure. Having only three beats in a measure gives waltz and Viennese waltz a distinct sound and feel, which can make the beat easier to hear.

A beat is the basic time unit in a piece of music. We use the beats to count in a song. Beats can be slower or faster or harder or softer than other beats, but that doesn't mean that they are given more or less value. In dance music, the beat usually stays consistent throughout the song, but if there is a live band, the beat is sometimes sped up or slowed down as the musicians interpret the music. All dance music can be played at different tempos regardless of the number of beats in a measure. However, the tempo (how fast or slow the song is) does not affect the number of beats per measure. Do not confuse beats per measure with another term, beats per minute. Beats per minute determine the tempo, while beats per measure tell us how to count the music.

> **D**ancing can reveal all the mystery that music conceals.
>
> *Charles Baudelaire, nineteenth-century French poet*

The beats are put together in a series of stronger and weaker beats, and this creates the measure of music. If the measure has three beats, we count the music 1, 2, 3. If the measure has 4 beats, then we count 1, 2, 3, 4. The first beat of the measure is called the *downbeat*, and it is the strongest beat. The name comes from the downward stroke of the conductor's baton as he or she leads musicians through a song. If beat 4 immediately precedes a new measure, it is called the *upbeat*, because the conductor's baton goes up to prepare for the downbeat. In music that is written in 4/4 time, the 1 beat (downbeat) is the strongest, the 3 beat is the next strongest, and the 2 and 4 are the weakest. The 2 and 4 beats are often called the *backbeat*, and even though they are the weaker beats, they are often accented musically with certain instruments. Because of this, the 2 beat and the 4 beat are the most natural time to clap your hands when listening to music. Various types of music will stress different beats to create a distinct sound or feeling to the music. To find the beats in the music, you have to listen to the bass line, which is created by a drum, a cymbal, or a bass guitar. The melody and singing will confuse you in the beginning, so it's best to ignore those extra sounds because they usually don't give a clear indication of the actual beat.

In dance language, we sometimes count in slows and quicks to make the timing easier to understand. That means we sometimes take only one step over the course of two beats of music. Saying *slow* represents two beats of music, and *quick* is one beat. So timewise, the slow is twice as long as the quick, or a slow takes the same amount of time as two quicks. For example, in foxtrot, some step patterns are counted slow, slow, quick, quick (which is six total beats, but only four steps), and others are slow, quick, quick (which is four beats, but only three steps). These differences in timing give the dances and the step patterns their own look and make for more rhythmic dancing. If there are more quicks in the step pattern, then that pattern moves faster than a pattern with a lot of slows in it. It's important to note, however, that the beat is consistent, even when we change the rhythm in some patterns by counting in slows and quicks. The timing for foxtrot and tango is explained in slows and quicks. Waltz and Viennese waltz always use the counts of the beats when counting, not slows and quicks. The beats are all even and counted 1, 2, 3. Because the Viennese waltz has a quicker tempo, the beats go by more quickly than in the slower waltz.

The Rate-a-Record segment on the popular and legendary television program *American Bandstand* popularized the phrase, "It's got a good beat, and it's easy to dance to." The beat, especially if it's driving and insistent, can make us want to get up and dance. Some people can feel the beat almost instinctively, especially if they have been brought up with a lot of music around them. But anyone can feel the beat with practice. To practice, listen to a type of music that is familiar, and clap your hands or tap your hand on a table or your lap to the beat. The best type of music to try this on is a strong disco-type beat because it is usually easy to feel the driving bass beat. If you're having trouble, have someone who does feel the beat listen to you count and guide you. They might have to clap along with you in the beginning until you get the feel of it. There are also Web sites that can help you understand music and rhythm through examples of music with different types of beats and rhythms.

After you can feel each beat, find the first beat of each measure, which is the 1 count. The 1 count is the downbeat, and it is the strongest count of each measure. Tap on count 1 on a table or your leg, then clap your hands for 2, 3, and 4. This exercise will help you to hear and feel the difference between the first beat in a measure and the other three beats.

The next step is to play the music that you will dance to from the DVD and find the beat and the 1 count. Again, tap a table on the 1 count, and then clap your hands on 2, 3, and 4 (see figure 3.1). The foxtrot and tango music are counted 1, 2, 3, 4. The waltz and Viennese waltz are counted 1, 2, 3, so tap on count 1 and clap your hands on 2 and 3 (see figure 3.2). Feeling the beat in the music is an important step in dancing because dancing and music go together. The music is part of the dance and the dance is part of the music. If you learn the step patterns but don't know how to put them to music (or even which music to put them to) then they will not be of much use to you. So, understanding how to identify not only the beat but also the first beat of the measure will help give you confidence on the floor when dancing. The music is the third dance partner, and both the man and the lady must be aware of it and understand its importance in the dance.

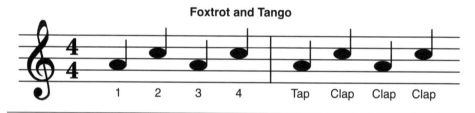

Figure 3.1   Time signature for the tango and foxtrot.

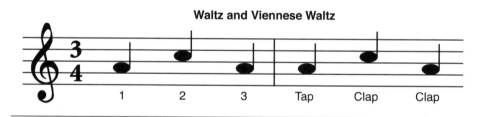

Figure 3.2   Time signature for the waltz and Viennese waltz.

DANCE-SPECIFIC BEATS

See this technique demonstrated on the DVD

Movement around the floor is the identifying trait of the ballroom dances. Each dance has its own characteristic that matches the music. Waltz has a sway and a characteristic rise-and-fall motion as it travels around the floor. The rise and fall is very smooth and graceful, not at all a jerky or abrupt movement. Waltz looks soft and gentle with a floating quality, but done at a high level, it is probably the most physically demanding of the ballroom dances. The music is written in 3/4 time, which means there are three beats to a bar of music. (Incidentally, this is not read as three-fourths time, but rather three-quarter time or three-four time.) Everything is counted in threes—1, 2, 3. Because in waltz there are only three beats in a measure, after count 3, count 1 starts again—1, 2, 3, 1, 2, 3. If you take a step on each beat, each measure of music will start with the opposite foot. So, a full box step (a basic pattern in the waltz) takes six counts, or two full measures, to complete. The 3/4 time signature is unique to waltz music; in fact, of all the ballroom and Latin dances, the only music written in 3/4 time are waltzes and Viennese waltzes. The strongest beat in waltz music is the 1; the 2 and 3 give a flowing feel. Even though the 1 is the strongest beat in waltz (the downbeat), do not feel that it is heavy in style. You must still feel the easy and gentle movement of the dance. Unless the dance is done to the older-style heavy Bavarian oom-pah band music, then the waltz is anything but heavy. You often hear many stringed instruments (such as violins) in waltz music because of their romantic quality. Even some contemporary musicians play waltz music. So, just because you hear a pop song, don't dismiss the idea of it being a waltz. Count it out. If it goes to 3 and starts over, then it's a waltz. The ideal waltz tempo for dancing is 84 to 128 beats per minute (bmp). The basic social steps in this book can be danced to the faster songs up to 128 bmp, but the intermediate step patterns should be danced to slower music, not faster than 90 bmp.

> **T**he one thing I tell people is when you're dancing just try to listen to the music and picture yourself, or assume that you're part of that band, that you're one of the instruments in that band, and you want to make your body do what that instrument is doing. And above all, enjoy yourself!
>
> *Frankie Manning, legendary swing dancer,* Dance Notes, *Vol. VI, Issue 2*

Tango is a walking dance that has a sharp turning action. The music usually has a dramatic flair, and is distinctly different from the other ballroom dances. The music itself has cultural influences from Africa, India, France, Spain, and Latin America. One of the things that sets it apart is that even though we think of and classify tango as a smooth dance, or ballroom dance, the music is very much affected by Latin sounds and character. Because of the origins of the dance, it carries with it a strong, passionate, and almost aggressive sound. Not a flighty dance, it is grounded and earthy in flavor, and the music demands deliberate movement. The music is written in 4/4 time (read as four-four time). That means there are four beats to a bar of music, counted 1, 2, 3, 4, and most of the time there is a unique rolling sound like a snare drum. Even though it is written in 4/4, to the dancer, tango music feels like it is grouped in eights. Each pattern in tango in this book is written in

good *musicality*. The music used in the ballroom dances is important to the way each dance is danced, but the feelings of the music leave the musicality open to individual interpretation. No one feels the same when a certain piece of music is played. One person might feel sad, another sexy, or dreamy, or nostalgic. There are probably as many emotions elicited by a certain piece of music as there are dancers. Even though each step taken has a certain beat value, each dancer might even feel the rhythm of the music differently. Just as musicians play the music a little differently depending on emotions and the other musicians, dancers express the dance any way they want to depending on their feelings and their partner. Once you have mastered identifying the beat and learning the step patterns, it is time to explore the music on an emotional and less technical level and allow that to color your dancing. This is where personal interpretation comes in. Don't forget, however, that this is not a substitute for dancing in time and to the beat. You must express yourself *through* the music, not in spite of it.

Learning
Ballroom Dancing

4

Posture and Movement

You just walked onto the dance floor with your partner and started moving to the music. The goal is to make it look like everything is easy and natural, like you've never taken a lesson. However, looking like a natural dancer requires an understanding of basic movement principles. More is involved in learning to dance than just knowing where to put your feet to do the step patterns. The body is what really dances, so it's important to know how to use the whole body correctly and efficiently. This chapter explains the basics of ballroom body movement, including posture, footwork, foot positions, and the direction to move around the floor. That will form the basis of the dances throughout this book.

POSTURE

One of the most important attributes of being a good dancer is understanding how to look confident on the floor. Looking good and gliding across the floor with confidence start with good posture. Standing up straight and letting the natural force of gravity do its work frees your body to move easily.

> **T**he steps cannot be learned without professional aid. But still we think, that while too much attention cannot be given to the learning of the steps, too little may be, and often is, bestowed upon the carriage of the figure.
>
> The Ball Room Annual, *1844*

Erect posture starts with lining up the vertebrae in the spine. The top of the spine, including the neck, to the tailbone should be in a relatively straight line. There is a small curve in the small of the back, but it should not be accentuated. Another way to think of it is that your torso is made up of three blocks: head, shoulders, and hips. The three blocks should always be in the same line. Your head should be extended above the spine and lifted high out of your shoulders (see figure 4.1).

To achieve good, erect posture, your abdominals must pull your midsection in. Many dance teachers use the phrase "keep your center" when referring to

Figure 4.1   Correct posture viewed from *(a)* the front and *(b)* the side.

keeping your midsection in. Sometimes it is a challenge to feel your abdominals pulled in, but understanding how to do it will make moving while dancing easier. One way to feel your midsection pulled in is to find the soft spot in the center of your body under your rib cage, and pull that soft spot up into your rib cage. If you can't find the spot, raise one arm high above your head and you'll feel that soft spot go into your rib cage as you reach. Another way to feel your abdominals pulling in is to imagine that you're pulling your belly button back to your spine.

There are different ways to check and practice good posture. One way is to stand with your back against a wall. Try to put your whole spine and back on the wall without curving your shoulders forward. For some people, this is difficult because so much time is spent sitting at desks working at computers or leaning forward to do aspects of their work. The top of the back becomes rounded and the small of the back very weak. For some people doing this exercise lying on the floor is a bit easier, because the bad habits of the body's posture are not as strong when lying down as when standing upright. When lying on the floor, keep the knees bent and the feet flat on the floor. In the beginning this might feel forced, but if you do this exercise every day for a few weeks, gradually the spine will begin to straighten out and you will start to feel natural in that position. Even though there is a slight curve in the small of the back, trying to straighten it out will make the abdominals and back muscles stronger. Another way to check your posture is to sit up straight on the edge

Figure 4.2 Posture is erect when sitting on a chair.

of a hard chair. When sitting up very straight, the posture is erect (see figure 4.2). Standing is usually the problem for most people. When standing, the alignment should stay the same in the upper body as when sitting, from the tailbone up to the top of the head.

If you feel your center needs strengthening or your posture needs improvement, you may find Pilates or the Alexander technique useful. Pilates strengthens and adds flexibility in the abdomen and the back areas. The Alexander technique, which is a movement-principle technique, is more study than exercise. It enhances posture and movement by teaching how the body is made so it can work efficiently. Teachers work individually with their students to help them feel and understand their own body and how to use it without putting unnecessary tension into it. Look into resources in your area if you think those programs would benefit you.

MOVING EASILY

Now that your posture is correct, you're ready to start moving while maintaining it. Most people walk without even thinking about how they actually do it. They stand erect, allow their body to move, and then their feet catch the body. Try walking normally, and you'll see that this is true. Or have someone give you a little push to knock you off balance. What happens? Your feet catch you. They don't let you fall down. These principles are evident when you watch a child learning to walk. There is coordination between the body traveling and the movement of the legs and feet to catch the body. We walk every day and never consider the way our legs move in time with the body. If we tried to analyze all of the muscles, ligaments, and physical forces involved in walking, most people would find it too complicated to comprehend and would suddenly start walking in a mechanical and unnatural manner. In her 1937 book *The Thinking Body*, Mabel E. Todd explains walking this way: "In walking, the weight is successively tumbling forward through all the body joints and being quickly met by the centering muscles to control it, and then the advancing leg swinging forward to support it." Everyone develops this sense naturally. But when those same people, who walk comfortably, get on the dance floor and put their arms up to dance, they look uncomfortable and awkward. They believe that dancing is different from walking. Their mind gets involved in how to move their body and legs instead of trusting that the body will do it naturally. When we walk, we don't consciously dissect how we get from one foot to the other; we just do it. In essence, we have the impulse to move, so we do. The same thing needs to happen when dancing. The dancer has to learn to trust that the body will walk from one foot to the other correctly. Even the size of the steps that we take when walking depends on the distance the body moves. The same is true when dancing. The more comfortable the dancers are with the step patterns, the more movement they will achieve, and the larger the steps will get.

The ballroom (or smooth) dances should travel around the floor, but the amount of movement depends on the experience of the dancers. Beginners will move considerably less than advanced dancers. When learning the steps, take a comfortable stride without trying to reach or extend your legs. The arms are held in what is called *dance position* when you ballroom dance, which also helps the balance of the two people dancing together. Dance position is described in the next chapter. There are also various body techniques and uses of the feet, which are explained in this chapter and also in chapter 5. These variants depend on the dance and step pattern. But dancing is really just walking to music. If you follow that important premise, learning to dance will be a relatively easy and enjoyable experience. This practice exercise will help make you aware of the natural action of the body when walking forward and backward.

Practice Exercise

Stand erect and walk forward and backward. Notice the way your legs move to catch your body. When walking forward, the moving leg will almost straighten in front of you, but when walking backward the moving leg will never straighten.

FOOTWORK

Footwork is the term used to explain the part of the foot that is in contact with the floor. Proper footwork enables dancers to move with their partner effectively, shows the character of the music, and adds to the fluidity of the movement. The terms used to describe footwork in this book are *flat foot* (or *whole foot*), *heel*, *ball of foot*, *toe*, *inside edge of the foot*, and *inside edge of the ball*. These terms are used in the explanations of each step pattern in the dances so you will know what part of the foot to use. Pictures show each of the footwork positions, and they are also listed for reader reference.

Flat foot (or whole foot).   The whole foot is flat on the floor. All dances use this foot position. It is the ending of each step pattern. The dancer stands on the whole foot to start the next pattern (see figure 4.3).

Figure 4.3   Flat foot.

Heel.   The padded back area of the foot. It is used only when the body weight is not completely on that foot. If you stand with your feet flat and roll back onto your heel while lifting the front part of the foot off the floor, that is the part of the heel that is used. The heel is the last part of the foot to leave the floor when walking backward and the first part to land on the floor when walking forward (see figure 4.4).

Figure 4.4   Heel.

Ball of foot. The rounded part of the foot between the arch and toe. The weight is positioned on the balls of the feet when the heels are raised (see figure 4.5).

Figure 4.5 Ball of foot.

Toe. The front part of the foot from the tips of the toes to the ball. This part of the foot is the first part of the foot on the floor when moving backward and sideward, and the last part on the floor when moving forward. There is no weight on it as it is moving. This term is also used on steps that rise, as in rise and fall, which are included in some of the dances in this book (see figure 4.6).

Figure 4.6 Toe.

Inside edge of the foot.   This term is used in tango and refers to the inside edge of the *whole foot*. Some steps move sideward and land on the inside edge of the foot before the weight is transferred to the foot (see figure 4.7).

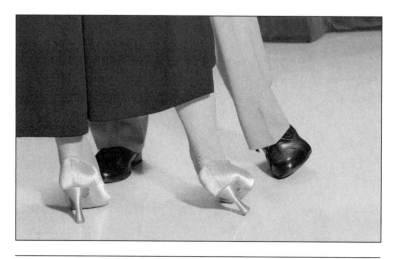

Figure 4.7   Inside edge of the foot.

Inside edge of the ball.   This is the inside edge of the *ball of the foot* only. Again, this term is used mainly in tango. Some tango steps end with drawing the foot toward the other foot with just the inside edge of the ball of the foot on the floor (see figure 4.8).

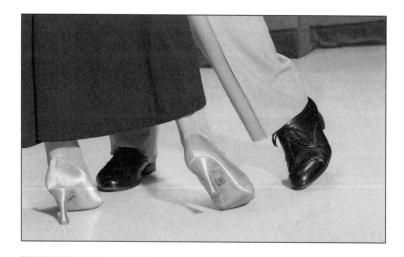

Figure 4.8   Inside edge of the ball.

Waltz, foxtrot, and Viennese waltz use the same principles for footwork because they are swing dances. There is a swinging motion of the body, which will be explained more in the next chapter. The term swing dances is used in the footwork section to refer to waltz, foxtrot, and Viennese waltz. Because of a swinging movement and a technique called *rise and fall*, there is a rolling through the foot from the front of the foot to the back on steps that move backward, and from the back of the foot to the front on steps that move forward. The feet don't land on the floor flat. The swinging of the body and the rise and fall create the correct footwork if danced properly. Side steps move to the side away from the foot that is supporting the weight, and almost always, the moving foot lands toe first.

Poetry is to prose as dancing is to walking.

John Wain, English novelist and poet

Beginners and advanced dancers need to be aware of the correct footwork. If the posture explained earlier is correct, the footwork has an almost natural feeling. The body will feel balanced and the movement easy without being forced. Effortless movement is what makes the dancer travel gracefully around the floor.

Practicing the exercises separately from the step patterns will help you understand the footwork and how to use your feet when moving forward, backward, and sideward. You will use the same foot movements, or footwork, when you dance the step patterns. The more you practice the footwork, the easier it will be to apply it to the step patterns.

> See this technique demonstrated on the DVD

Practice Exercise:
Forward and Backward Walks for Swing Dances

To practice forward walks, start by standing with the feet parallel to each other, a couple of inches apart. Begin by taking a step forward with the left foot. When walking forward, the first part of the moving foot to hit the floor is the heel, and then the foot goes to flat. As you continue to move forward, the foot will roll through the ball of the foot, and finally off the toe as the weight shifts to the other foot. This is the forward movement used for almost all forward steps. Make sure your feet do not turn out. They should remain parallel to each other throughout the walk. Remember to keep the hip, knee, and ankle joints relaxed and the upper body erect. Repeat the exercise stepping with the right foot first.

Walking backward is just the opposite. Start with the feet parallel to each other, a couple of inches apart. Take a step by pointing the toe of the right foot back, roll to ball, then flat, and release off the heel as the weight shifts back onto the left foot, which begins your next step. Normally when the feet are passing through the point where they are together, both feet are flat. This foot action is used in most backward moving steps. Make sure your feet do not turn out. They should remain parallel to each other throughout the walks. Remember again to keep the hip, knee, and ankle joints relaxed and the posture erect. Practice this same exercise by stepping first with the left foot.

Practice Exercise:
Side Steps for Swing Dances That Have Rise

An exercise for side steps is to rise up on the balls of both feet and walk around like that just to get the feel of that part of the foot. Then stand flat on the left foot with feet together, slide the toe of the right foot to the side, put your weight on the ball of the right foot, and slide the left foot to meet it. When the feet come together lower the left foot flat to the floor. Keep the hip, knee, and ankle joints relaxed and the posture erect. Practice this same exercise with the other foot. This movement is used for all side steps that rise.

Practice Exercise:
Side Steps for Swing Dances That Do Not Rise

In foxtrot there is no rise after the side step is taken, so the foot will go flat before the other foot meets it. Stand flat on the left foot with feet together, slide the toe of the right foot to the side, put your weight on a flat right foot, and slide the left foot to meet it. Keep the hip, knee, and ankle joints relaxed and the posture erect. Practice this same exercise with the other foot. This same movement is used for all side steps in foxtrot.

Tango is completely different from the swing dances and therefore requires unique footwork. There is no rise and fall in tango, so only the ball of the foot is used instead of the toe. All forward steps walk with a heel and then go flat very quickly, so the feet do not roll as in the swing dances. The moving foot is picked up, just clearing the floor. Backward steps are ball, heel, and again the moving foot is picked up and moved backward to the ball. Side steps are normally ball, flat, but there are times when the inside of the feet are used—the inside edge of the whole foot and the inside edge of the ball.

Practice Exercise:
Forward and Backward Walks in Tango

To practice forward walks, start with the feet parallel to each other, a couple of inches apart. Step forward with the left foot, lifting it off the floor about a quarter of an inch. The first part of the foot to hit the floor is the heel, and then the foot goes to flat just like in the swing dances, but in tango the foot does not continue to roll. Keep the hip, knee, and ankle joints relaxed and the posture erect. Practice this same exercise stepping forward with the right foot first. This walk is the same for all forward walks in tango.

To practice backward walks, start with the feet parallel to each other, a couple of inches apart. Step backward with the right foot, lifting the foot off the floor about a quarter of an inch. The first part of the right foot to hit the floor is the ball. Quickly move to a flat foot and release the heel of the left foot. Again, there is no rolling of the foot as in the swing dances; the feet remain as flat as possible. Keep the hip, knee, and ankle joints relaxed and the posture erect. Practice this same exercise stepping backward with the left foot first. This walk is the same on all backward walks in tango.

Practice Exercise: Side Steps in Tango

Stand with the left foot flat, pick up your right foot and place it to the side with only the inside edge of the right foot on the floor. Flatten the right foot, pick up the left foot, and place it flat next to the right foot. Keep the hip, knee, and ankle joints relaxed and the posture erect. Practice this same exercise with the opposite foot. This footwork is used on some side steps in tango.

Side steps that drag the toe are a bit different. To practice these, stand on the left foot and then step to the side with the right foot. Drag the inside of the ball of the left foot toward the right foot until the tops of the legs touch each other. Keep the hip, knee, and ankle joints relaxed and the posture erect. Practice this exercise with the opposite foot. This footwork is used at the end of many of the tango step patterns.

FOOT POSITION

Also important to ballroom dance is foot position. Foot position refers to where you put your foot on the floor in relation to the other foot. To accomplish the step patterns in this book, understanding the direction and placement of the feet is important for correctly moving with your partner and around the floor. Forward is directly forward from wherever you are facing or where your belly button is facing. Most of the time, the body faces the same direction as the feet, but in some of the step patterns, the body faces a different direction than the feet. The term *foot position* always refers to where the feet face, even if the body faces a different direction. Back is directly behind where your feet are. Each step pattern notes the foot placement of each step.

An effective way to envision foot position is to imagine a clock lying on the floor, and you are standing in the center of the clock facing the 12. Back would be toward the 6, side to the right would be toward the 3, and side to the left would be toward the 9. Other foot positions are a little more complicated and are approximate. Refer to the foot-position diagram to understand these positions (see figure 4.9).

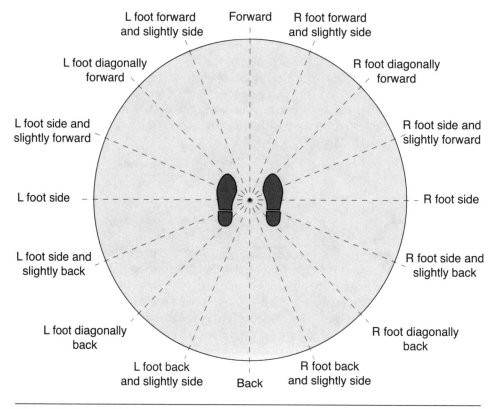

Figure 4.9 Foot positions.

CONTRARY BODY MOVEMENT POSITION

See this technique demonstrated on the DVD

Contrary body movement position, or CBMP, is a foot position. Sometimes, you may hear this referred to as contra body movement position. CBMP is placing the stepping foot in the same line and in front of or behind the standing foot. CBMP is used on step patterns that go to outside partner position in waltz, foxtrot, and tango. It enables the couple to stay in closed dance position while stepping with the foot in outside position. Closed and outside position are explained in chapter 5. In the dance chapters, CBMP is noted in the specific step patterns in which it is used.

In tango, CBMP is also used on most forward steps with the left foot and back steps with the right foot. On forward steps with the left foot, the left thigh crosses the right thigh. The right foot then steps forward with the right side of the body leading, so the thighs are open. Going backward, the right foot walks back in CBMP, or in the same line as the left foot. Then the left foot steps back with the left side leading. Normally the man is walking forward and the lady backward. This foot position causes the dance to curve strongly to the left, which is one of the characteristics of the tango. Tango is a very flat dance that uses turning movements and changes of speed to make it look different from the swing dances. CBMP helps to accomplish this look.

These practice exercises will help you understand the main characteristic of tango, which curves as it moves in a forward direction. When you are first learning the tango step patterns, it is best not to put the CBMP in the dance. Take the time to understand all of the other aspects of the patterns first. When comfortable with the patterns, start using CBMP to curve the forward and backward steps. In the tango chapter, CBMP is noted in the specific places in the step patterns that it is used.

Practice Exercise:
Applying CBMP to Tango

Forward Walks: Step 1

Stand facing a mirror with the weight on your right foot. Turn the shoulders to the left as you step straight forward with the left foot in a turned-out position, which means that the foot is turned out away from the ankle at about a 45-degree angle. You'll see in the mirror that the left foot is in the same line as your right foot. That happens because of the turnout of your left foot and the turn of the shoulders. This foot position is CBMP. Remember to keep your ankle, knee, and hip joints relaxed and your spine erect.

Forward Walks: Step 2

Stand with your left foot forward in CBMP. You will see that your belly button is now turned slightly leftward from where you started. From that position, step forward with your right foot, keeping your shoulders turned left. This is right foot forward with right side leading. Remember to keep your ankle, knee, and hip joints relaxed and your spine erect.

Backward Walks: Step 1

Stand facing a mirror with your weight on your left foot. Turn your right foot inward as you walk straight back on it. Your right foot will be directly under your center, or in the same line as your left foot. This is CBMP as well. Remember to keep your ankle, knee, and hip joint relaxed and your spine erect.

Backward Walks: Step 2

Stand with your right foot back in CBMP. You will see that your belly button is turned leftward slightly. From that position, step back with the left foot, keeping the same amount of body turn. This is left foot back with left side leading. Remember to keep your ankle, knee, and hip joints relaxed and your spine erect.

Putting the left and right steps together will create a curving to the left.

DIRECTIONS OF MOVEMENT

See this technique demonstrated on the DVD

The direction you move around the floor is essential in the ballroom dances. In dance terminology it is called *line of dance*. The line of dance moves counterclockwise around the floor, so the dancers move in that direction as they dance the step patterns (see figure 4.10). This directional movement around the floor goes back centuries to when men wore swords while dancing. Because most men were right handed, they wore the sword and scabbard on the left to facilitate drawing the sword with the right hand. So, the lady had to be on the man's right side to keep from tripping over the sword. For a promenade, or walking step, around the floor, the man would take the inside of the turn so as not to hit the legs of the audience around the floor with his sword; therefore, the lady would be on the man's right side, or the outside edge of the floor. To proceed forward, they had to promenade counterclockwise. This directional line of dance remains with us in the modern ballroom dances, even though men rarely wear swords to dances today!

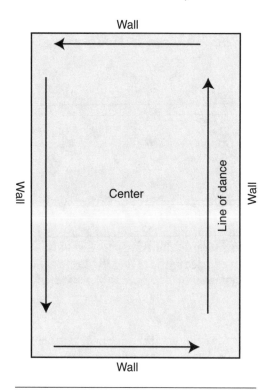

Wall

Wall

Center

Line of dance

Wall

Wall

Figure 4.10　Line of dance.

As you begin to learn the dances in this book, all of the instructions may be overwhelming, so take your time and study one section at a time. The first thing the beginning dancer needs to know is that dancing on a ballroom floor is like driving a car on the highway. Moving in the wrong direction around the floor would be like driving your car against traffic—very dangerous. Cars move in the same general direction, but they change lanes, slow down, and sometimes even stop to avoid running into another car. Because the dances in this book are all ballroom dances, they move around the floor, and there is very little opportunity to stay in one place. Latin dances—such as cha cha and rumba—stay in one place on the floor for the most part, but a characteristic of ballroom, or smooth, dances is progressive movement. So understanding the alignments is essential to dancing these dances, and a lot of practical knowledge is needed. Just learning it by looking in the book is almost impossible. You must get up and actually try the directional changes, being aware that another couple may be where you want to go next. There are always other dancers moving in and out of your way, just like driving on a highway.

Each step pattern also moves in its own direction within the counterclockwise movement of the dance. Those directions are noted with each pattern. A few step patterns are stationary, but they should only be used to avoid a collision with another couple that gets in the way, which is also explained with each step pattern. These step patterns are sometimes called *evasive steps*.

Terms used when talking about alignments are: *line of dance, center, wall, diagonal wall*, and *diagonal center*. These help dancers orient themselves to specific parts of the room.

Other terms, such as *facing, backing, pointing*, and *against*, indicate the direction the dancer is moving and turning. The following puts the directions and alignments together: If you're standing toward the outside of the dance floor facing the line of dance (facing the counterclockwise line you will be moving on), to your left is called *center of the room* and to your right *wall of the room*. Turning your feet 45 degrees to the left from line of dance puts you facing *diagonal center*, and turning your feet 45 degrees to the right from line of dance puts you facing *diagonal wall*.

If you turn your body 180 degrees from where you were facing, you are *backing line of dance*. From this position, turning your feet 45 degrees to the left puts you *backing diagonal center*, and turning your feet 45 degrees to the right puts you *backing diagonal wall*. To help you better understand these terms, figure 4.11 provides a visual representation of the dance alignments.

The term *against* means that you are moving backward against the counterclockwise movement of the dance. *Against* can be used for any of the

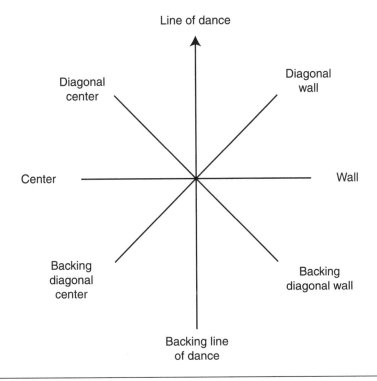

Figure 4.11 Dance alignments.

alignments: center, wall, diagonal, or line of dance. The term *pointing* is used when the dancer is on the inside of a turn. This only happens when you are the person moving backward. So, on the back half of a turning step pattern, the foot points in the direction of travel (see figure 4.12). When *pointing* is stated, it also means that the body faces a different direction than the foot does.

As was mentioned earlier, the alignments noted in the step patterns always indicate where the feet are facing, not where the body is facing. Most of the time it is the same, but there are some cases in which the body faces a different direction than the feet.

Figure 4.12 Pointing.

Practice Exercise: Finding Alignments

Stand in a place that you can imagine a dance floor. Find line of dance, center, wall, diagonal center, and diagonal wall for each of the four walls on your dance floor and face forward to these alignments. After that, face backward to these alignments.

CHAPTER 5

Two People Dancing as One

*T*he ultimate goal in ballroom dancing is to find a physical and emotional connection to a partner so that the two bodies move together effortlessly. There should be joy and an attitude of fun in the movement. The dance couple has its own character and distinctiveness, which complement each person's individual qualities. Dancing with a partner should be an enjoyable and shared experience between the two people involved in the partnership, whether that partnership is just for one dance or many dances. Making each other look good on the dance floor is what ballroom dancing is all about.

This chapter focuses on the tools needed to dance with a partner. All of the tools are important, but understanding the roles of the leader and follower is essential. For two bodies to move together as one, one person decides what the couple is going to do and the other person follows that lead, so leading and following are explained first. The next aspect explained is the importance of dance position and its use in leading and following. Correct dance position must be maintained to accomplish the step patterns comfortably. Also explained in this chapter is learning how to turn the two bodies together. Most of the step patterns have some turn within the pattern, and knowing how to turn makes the dancing easier. Waltz, foxtrot, and Viennese waltz use the elements of rise and fall, swing, and sway as characteristics of the dances. These elements are more like the icing on the cake. They're not necessary to accomplish the step patterns, but they show the musicality and feeling of the dance. They are also explained in detail.

PARTNERING SKILLS

Since ballroom dancing first became fashionable, there have been many social changes in Western society. Chapter 1 described the different eras and their impact on partner dancing. Most people consider that modern partner dancing began in the Renaissance era, or the 1600s. During that time, and indeed throughout most of history, men were traditionally seen to be the leaders of the household. They were the ones who made the decisions, took care of the women, and were the head of the family. The women stayed home and cooked, cleaned, took care of the kids, and were not very involved in business or major decision making. So the men were naturally the leaders on the dance floor and women the followers. But quotes from dance manuals during the nineteenth century show a great respect for women as dance partners. In 1847, America's most famous dance master at the time, Charles Durang, said, "Gentlemen ought always to be attentive to their partners, and they should move in unison with their every step and attitude." Another dance master, Professor Maas, was quoted in 1871 as saying, "In general manners, both ladies and gentlemen should act as though the other person's happiness was of as much importance as their own."

The 1920s brought a different attitude to the dance floor—during this period the term *lead* meant command and *follow* meant obey. This attitude shift began right around the time that women earned the right to vote. Dance manuals started referring to the partners as *man* and *girl*, and the woman was told to adjust to the man. If there was a problem, it was considered to be her fault. Explanations in the manuals started saying things like, "making her do the step" and "controlling the movement of the girl." The attitude in ballroom dancing was that the men controlled and the women were submissive.

That was fairly common thinking until the 1960s when the societal roles of men and women changed. Women started to be more independent and enjoyed making their own decisions; some men started staying home to take care of the house and kids. In today's society, there is much more equality between men and women. So the roles of the leader and follower seem outdated, but ballroom dancing began when those antiquated beliefs were the norm. Today, there are still two people in a dance partnership, but they each have their own minds and are used to making their own decisions. If both partners tried to be the leader, the dance would never work; it would always be a struggle. So dancing successfully with a partner still requires just one person making the decisions. Just like in the 1600s, it is the man's job to lead and the lady's job to follow, but only on the dance floor!

It's difficult for many women in this day and age to identify with the words *lead* and *follow*. Women want to be considered equals; they don't want to feel that they are less important, and the word *follow* implies just that. Both the man and the woman are equally important in a partnership, and that equality is essential in developing a good partnership. Dancing is a shared experience. The two people dancing together contribute to each other. So a more appropriate way of saying it is that the man creates an action and the lady responds to his action. The man asks the lady to do something, and if asked correctly, the lady will respond in such a way that the two bodies move together effectively.

The man's role in the partnership is to decide the step pattern, timing, direction, and how much he wants to move. The step pattern is the particular pattern the man would like to dance at that particular time. Timing includes the musicality and beat values he chooses. Direction is where the man wants to move on the floor, which is determined by the dance traffic. The distance he wants to move depends on the number of dancers on the floor and the size of the floor. The man's jobs are mostly mental. He has all the decisions to make, and then must convey his thoughts correctly to the woman. He proposes a certain way of moving, but not in a controlling way. The man indicates what he wants to do mainly by a clear change of his weight from one foot to the other. He does not pull or push the woman. But his arms must be in a good dance position, which will be explained in the next section, so the woman can feel the changes. In some instances, the man will use his hands to turn the woman. But because the dances in this book are ballroom dances, the couple stays in closed dance position most of the time, and the change of his weight is the most important factor.

Dancing is a wonderful training for girls, it's the first way you learn to guess what a man is going to do before he does it.

Christopher Morley, American novelist and journalist

The woman's role is to respond to the man's action. Her body and her mind have to be ready to do whatever the man asks her to do; she cannot anticipate what is going to happen. She has to know the timing and the step patterns, but must not consciously think of the patterns, the timing, or where she's going as they are dancing. If she thinks about it, then she will do the patterns and timing that she wants to do, not necessarily what the man wants to do. The woman will eventually move instinctively with the man. She responds to what the man asks her to do, which is an extremely important part of the partnership. Sometimes women will say, "If I have a good leader, I can follow anything." But that is not completely true. The lady does have to learn how to respond to the man just as much as the man has to learn how to make the action. The woman is not just standing in dance position smiling and batting her eyes. She uses her mental faculties to make her body respond and perform the physical actions appropriately. The man never moves the lady. She is self-propelled and moves herself across the floor in the confines of the man's frame, moving her feet as the man moves and changes his weight. The woman also supports her own weight and doesn't lean on her partner.

All the couples that have been at the top have had a strong woman. She's not just hanging on being a pretty face.

Maja Servé, world professional standard finalist, Dance Notes, Vol. II, Issue 5

An open line of communication between the two partners is imperative for the dancing to work. If both partners are trained correctly, they are equal and they should dance as equals That is the beauty of watching good dancing and also being a part of it. Because the lady is not really under the man's control, there is a feeling of spontaneity, which is appealing to the audience and makes the dancing fun for the partners.

Two people dancing together are controlled by two different minds, each with his or her own motivation, interpretations, and strengths. So being able to move easily with a partner takes practice and an understanding of the principles in this chapter. It is probably the most difficult aspect of dancing for the beginner, but with a little practice it is well worth the effort. If you and your partner are having trouble moving together, go back to the previous chapter and make sure that your posture is correct. Erect posture will fix most problems. If it is still not working, check that the arms are in the correct dance position and make sure that the man is changing his weight completely. If the woman still cannot feel where the man is going, then go back to the practice exercises in this chapter to review the feel of partnering each other.

The only way to develop good communication on the dance floor is to use the practice exercises in this chapter. These exercises will develop the role of the man in terms of creating an action and the role of the woman in responding to that action. Dancing with a partner takes practice; it's much more than just memorizing the step patterns.

DANCE POSITIONS

Dance position is the way the couple holds their bodies and arms in relation to each other as they dance the various patterns. Staying in the correct dance position is the only way that two people can move together easily. As

Practice Exercise: Moving as One

Figure 5.1   Holding hands at waist level.

Stand facing your partner, holding hands. The hands should be held at about waist level (see figure 5.1). As the man moves in different directions changing his weight completely from foot to foot, the woman responds with the weight changes. This develops a feeling between the partners—the man of changing his weight and the lady of moving her body and feet with that weight change. The lady closes her eyes if possible. When the woman closes her eyes during this exercise, two things happen: The woman relies only on the feel of the man's movement because she cannot receive visual clues from him, and the man finds he must move in a definite manner for the lady to respond accordingly. In the beginning it might be a bit awkward, but after a few times, it becomes fun and is useful for developing response skills.

mentioned earlier, dance position is an important element in partner dancing because the woman has to feel when the man is changing his weight so she can move with him. This book covers three major dance positions: closed position, outside position, and promenade position. These are used in the various step patterns, so understanding these body positions will make learning the step patterns easier. Some of the patterns use more than one of these positions; understanding them and how to move from one to the other is important to the flow of the dancing.

Closed Position

Closed dance position is the position used most in the ballroom dances. Think of closed dance position as home base. Closed dance position is the same for waltz, foxtrot, and Viennese waltz. Tango closed position is a little different, but when first learning tango, the regular closed position should be used.

> See this technique demonstrated on the DVD

In closed position, the couple is face to face, with their bodies parallel to each other. They are slightly offset rather than in line with each other, with the center of the lady's body (where her sternum is located) lined up with and facing the man's right front. If the man were wearing suspenders, his right front would be the right suspender. Another way to look at it is that the man's right foot will travel between the lady's feet as they move, because the two bodies are offset (see figure 5.2). Because the lady is slightly toward the right side of the man's body, her right foot will travel between the man's feet.

The position of the hands, arms, and heads is called the topline of the partnership. In closed position, the man's right hand is cupped with fingers and thumb closed around the lady's left shoulder blade on her back. His right elbow is positioned on a slight slope downward from the shoulder, at a height halfway between the top and bottom of the lady's sternum. The lady puts her left hand on the man's right arm, with her thumb and second finger cupping the bicep, which is the muscle on the front of the upper arm.

Figure 5.2   The man's right foot travels between the lady's feet as they move.

The man's left hand holds the lady's right hand between his thumb and first finger. It is raised to about the lady's nose level with a slight slope downward in his upper arm. The elbow is bent to nearly a right angle and is in line with his back. The woman's right elbow is relaxed. The arms of both partners should remain steady. The arm and hand position should remain the same throughout the dance.

The man's head is turned left and looks at the 11:00 position. The weight of his head is toward his left foot. The lady's head is also toward her left side but is positioned on an angle tilted somewhat toward her left elbow, which creates a longer line for the topline. See figure 5.3 for various views of the closed position.

Figure 5.3 Proper execution of closed position.

Outside Position

Outside position is another dance position used in the ballroom dances. In this book, waltz, tango, and foxtrot use this position in various step patterns. Two types of outside position will be referred to: right outside position and left outside position. Right outside position is when the man's right foot moves to the outside of the lady's right foot instead of between her feet (see figure 5.4a). In left outside position the man's left foot moves to the outside of the lady's left foot (see figure 5.4b).

Figure 5.4 *(a)* Right outside position and *(b)* left outside position.

See this technique demonstrated on the DVD

Outside position is only from the middle of the thigh down to the foot. The body is still in closed position in the arms, hands, and head positions. The integrity of the topline should be maintained. In the beginning levels of dance, this position is only maintained for one or two steps. As dancers become more advanced, it is easier to stay in this position. Contrary body movement (CBM) is another tool needed to dance in outside position comfortably and will make outside position easier to achieve. It is explained in the next section.

Promenade Position

See this technique demonstrated on the DVD

Promenade position is a body position in which both partners move forward in the same direction. In this position, both partners can see where they are going, because neither one is moving backward.

It is a position used in many of the step patterns in all of the ballroom dances. In this book, however, promenade position is only used in step patterns in waltz, tango, and foxtrot. The arm and hand positions remain the same as in closed position, but the feet form a 90-degree angle between the partners so they can both move forward at the same time. Both the man and woman turn their heads to face the direction they are moving, which is the direction that the feet are facing. The shoulders form a 45-degree angle between the partners. The connecting hands are held directly between the shoulders of the two partners and point in the direction of the movement (see figure 5.5).

Figure 5.5 Promenade position.

Closed Position for Tango

See this technique demonstrated on the DVD

In the closed position for tango, the lady will be slightly more to the man's right than in the other dances. This places his right arm more around her body so his fingers will probably be on her spine. The exact placement will vary depending on the size of the woman and the length of the man's right arm. His right arm is also lower than in the other dances because of the unique placement of her left arm. His elbow should be at the height of the bottom of the lady's sternum. The man's left elbow is slightly higher than in the other dances, with the palm of his hand turned to face his partner.

The lady's left arm is the tricky part. She places her elbow on top of the man's elbow with her palm facing her body. This can be uncomfortable if not placed correctly. The elbows of the man and lady should feel connected. The lady's right hand is placed in the man's left, with her elbow hanging from the hand. Refer to figure 5.6 for various views of proper positioning. You can see that this dance position is a little more advanced, so dancing tango in the closed dance position used for waltz, foxtrot, and Viennese waltz is much easier, and it is just as effective until you get to the higher levels of dancing.

Figure 5.6 Proper execution of the tango closed position.

Practice Exercises: Tango Arm Positioning

Exercise #1

This exercise demonstrates the position of the man's right arm for tango. Both partners stand with good posture. The gentleman puts his right arm in position with his hand directly in front of his belly button. This is approximately where his hand will be. The lady puts her body between the man's hand and his body in her dance position. Take forward, back, and side steps in this position.

Exercise #2

This exercise demonstrates the lady's left arm position for tango. Both partners stand with good posture. The gentleman extends his right arm straight in front of him. The lady drapes her left elbow over his elbow, with her hand hanging straight down on a right angle from her elbow. The lady now rotates her wrist leftward until the palm of her hand faces her as she steps forward into position. The man bends his elbow and puts it into dance position. There should be a connection between the two elbows, and the lady's fingertips will touch the man's back right under his arm pit. Move forward, back, and side in this position.

Once both partners are comfortable in this tango position, walk around until it's easy to move together. Then you can try to dance the step patterns. Outside and promenade positions in tango are danced in this same position. But remember to use the regular closed dance position if this position is not comfortable for you.

TURNING TECHNIQUES

Most of the step patterns in ballroom dancing involve some turning of the bodies. Turn means to revolve or to rotate. So, in dance terminology, turn means that the couple turns to face a different direction from where they started. The turn can be done at various times, at various speeds, and in various amounts. This all depends on the step pattern being executed. Each step pattern turns differently, which is one of the variables that make the step patterns different from one another. Most of the time, the turn is done by both bodies at the same time, but there are a few instances when only one of the bodies turns. To turn both bodies together, the couple must keep an erect posture, described in chapter 4, and a good closed dance position. The erect posture and balanced dance position keep the bodies in the correct placement so the turn can be accomplished. The next element that makes turning the bodies more comfortable is contrary body movement.

Contrary Body Movement

Contrary body movement, referred to as CBM, is a body action used to initiate a turn. It is turning the body around the spine and is mainly used on forward and backward steps. No CBM is used on side steps. CBM involves turning the opposite side of the body toward the stepping foot if moving in a forward direction. Or one can think of it as the natural way the body moves when walking. As the left foot walks forward, the right arm and side of the body move forward, and when the right foot walks forward, the left arm and left side of the body move forward.

> See this technique demonstrated on the DVD

When moving in a backward direction, CBM involves turning the moving foot inward. For dancing purposes, each person within the partnership has to use different parts of the body to make the turn work. The person going forward is considered to be on the outside of the turn or rotation so that the turn is split over a certain number of steps, depending on the step pattern. That person will turn the upper body just like when walking. The person going backward is on the inside of the turn or rotation so all the turn is made between the step back and the following step. That's the reason the foot is turned inward. If the partner on the inside of the turn turns too much, the person on the outside of the turn will not be able to move to the place he or she needs to.

> **T**he most important thing in a partnership is the ability to work together and realize you are a team working toward one common goal.
>
> *Glenn Weiss, world professional standard finalist,*
> Dance Notes, *July/August 1998*

To help understand the terminology in the chapters that explain the dances, chapters 6 through 9, and to explain back steps more clearly, most back steps that turn will be written with the second step of the step pattern pointing in a certain direction with the body turning less than the foot. On the next step, the body catches up to the amount that the foot is turned so the whole body, including the feet, end facing the same direction. In some of the patterns, you will notice that the man and the lady do a different amount of turn on the same step. This is because the amount of turn is dependent on which partner is on the inside and which is on the outside of the turn.

These practice exercises will help you understand how to initiate the turn of your own body moving backward and forward. As explained earlier, turning the bodies at the correct times is the only way the two bodies can move together comfortably in dance position. You'll know if you are doing it correctly if there is an ease of movement and if your positions match those in the photos and DVD.

Practice Exercise: CBM Forward and Backward

To practice CBM moving forward, without your partner, walk forward and feel the way your arms swing opposite of the leg that is moving. When your left foot is moving forward, your right arm is swinging forward, and when your right foot is moving forward, your left arm is swinging forward. Next, take a step forward with your left foot and swing your right arm forward so the body turns to the left (see figure 5.7). Then take a step forward with the right foot and swing your left arm forward so the body turns to the right.

To practice CBM moving backward, stand facing a mirror with your feet about three inches (7.6 cm) apart. Put all your weight on your right foot and step backward with your left foot while turning your toe inward (see figure 5.8). As your left foot moves backward, maintain the same distance (3 inches [7.6 cm]) between the feet as in the starting position. Then stand completely on the left foot with your back straight, point your right foot to the side, and transfer all of your weight onto the right foot, remembering to keep your back straight at all times. The feet will end up facing from one-eighth of a turn to one-quarter of a turn to the right of where they began. For this practice exercise, the amount of turn is not important. The purpose is to help you understand how to move your body backward as it is turning. Do the same exercise with the other foot moving backward. You will notice that when walking backward, your moving leg will not straighten.

Figure 5.7   CBM moving forward.

Figure 5.8   CBM moving backward.

Opening to Promenade Position

Promenade position was explained earlier in this chapter. It always begins from a closed dance position and it is used to dance various step patterns. Dancing in promenade position is always a fun and relatively easy variation that looks like a more advanced step pattern.

See this technique demonstrated on the DVD

There are two ways of turning the bodies to promenade position. One is opening to the right and the other opening to the left. The two ways to get to promenade are determined by the step pattern that the couple is dancing and which direction the man wants to move. So if the man wants to move toward the center of the room, he will open to the left to get to promenade position, and if he wants to go toward the wall, he will open to the right to get to promenade position. When opening to the right, the man turns his upper body to the right as the lady turns her feet to the right. When opening to the left, the man turns his feet to the left as the lady turns her upper body to the left.

The man's right hand and wrist are also used to convey promenade position to the woman. The man's right hand will always face the direction that he wants the lady's feet to face. When opening to the right, immediately after the man turns his upper body to the right, his right wrist will flex backward so there is room for the lady to turn her feet. When opening to the left, the man's right hand will stay facing the same direction, but he turns his feet away from the hand. No matter which way is used, the foot position between the man and lady will end up being at a 90-degree angle to each other, and the shoulders of the man and lady at a 45-degree angle to each other. The direction of travel will be on the line where their hands are pointing.

Getting the lady back to closed position varies and depends on the step pattern being danced. Sometimes the man closes his feet back to the woman, and other times the man closes the woman's feet back to him. When the man closes the woman, he always uses his right hand and wrist to turn her body to face him in closed position.

Practice Exercise:
Opening to Promenade to the Left and Right

To practice opening to promenade to the right, stand in closed dance position. The man turns his upper body to the right about one-eighth of a turn without turning his feet. The man's right hand and wrist will also turn so that they follow the lady's body. The lady turns her feet a quarter of a turn without turning her upper body. The result is promenade position—feet at a 90-degree angle and the shoulders at a 45-degree angle.

To practice opening to promenade to the left, stand in closed dance position. The man turns his feet to the left about a quarter of a turn without turning his upper body. The lady turns her upper body left and not her feet. The result is promenade position—feet at a 90-degree angle and the shoulders at a 45-degree angle.

STYLING

See this technique demonstrated on the DVD

Other body movements will help you express the music more fully and will make your dancing more enjoyable to watch. These are styling techniques and include rise and fall, swing, and sway. These techniques are not necessary for dancing the step patterns, but they will make the dance look and feel more complete.

Rise and Fall

See this technique demonstrated on the DVD

Rise is increased elevation in the feet, knees, and body. Fall is lowering from the toe to heel on the supporting foot. This rising and falling motion is more evident in the waltz than in any other dance, but

Practice Exercise: Rise and Fall

This exercise will help you become comfortable with the position of the body and feet during the rise portion of the rise and fall used in the waltz. Because we are not used to standing on the balls of our feet, this movement needs to be experienced. With practice, it will become a natural movement for your body, and it will be easier to put into the actual step patterns.

Stand with erect posture, with a slight flex in the hip joint, the knee joint, and the ankles. This is called neutral position (see figure 5.9). Now stretch your head and spine upward and raise your heels off the ground until you are on the balls of your feet. Walk around on that cushiony part of your foot to get used to it. This is your rise. You will never be any higher than that (see figure 5.10). Go back down to neutral then stretch your body up again and walk around. Refer to chapter 4 for an explanation of the various parts of the foot.

Figure 5.9 The neutral position.

Figure 5.10 Rising to the balls of the feet.

there is also rise and fall in the foxtrot and Viennese waltz. Several types of rise and fall are used in all three dances, and the specifics are explained in the appropriate chapter. This practice exercise will help you understand the feeling of rise and fall.

Swing

Waltz, foxtrot, and Viennese waltz include the element of swing in their movements; that is the reason they are called swing dances, which was first explained in chapter 4. These three dances have a different feel to them than the tango, which is really just a walking dance with no rise and fall. Swinging the body creates a feeling of freedom in the movement of the body. But what does swing mean? Swing is movement around a fixed point, like a pendulum. Different parts of the body swing in these three dances. When walking, the leg moves from the hip joint, so the hip joint is the fixed point and the leg is swinging. In a body swing, the head is the fixed point and the body swings under it (see figure 5.11).

> See this technique demonstrated on the DVD

Of course, when you're moving, the head is not at a fixed point in the room, but it is the fixed point of the body swing. This element might be a little complicated right now, but it is included for your general knowledge because the next element explained is sway. Most of the time the body has to have a swinging movement to create the sway.

These practice exercises will help you feel the swinging movements in your body so that your dancing will become more free. If possible, do these exercises in front of a full-length mirror standing sideways. It will be the most beneficial if you can see your body and how it is standing and moving.

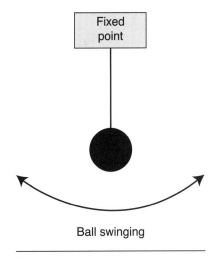

Figure 5.11 Body swing.

Practice Exercise: Swing

Leg Swing

Stand on one leg and let the other leg swing back and forth under your body. Your hips should remain still and fixed with the trunk of your body, and your spine erect. The leg is the only thing moving, and it is swinging from the hip. When it swings in front of you the knee will be straight but when it swings behind you it will be flexed, which is a natural movement. This is leg swing.

Body Swing

Keep your head fixed and move your body from the sternum area and down to your feet forward and backward under your head. This is body swing.

Sway

See this technique demonstrated on the DVD

Waltz, foxtrot, and Viennese waltz all use sway. Sway is the natural inclination of the body toward the inside of the turn or away from the moving foot. It can be used for balance, but is mostly for effect. The swaying of the body makes the dance look more fluid and elegant. To dance a sway correctly, there must be a swing of the body, which was explained in the previous section. A sway should not be just a broken bend at the waist, but rather come as a result of the movement.

To dance a sway, one side of the upper body has to be stretched higher than the other side. A sway to the right means that the left side of the upper body is stretched higher than the right side, like a tilt of the body to the right. A sway to the left means that the right side of the upper body is stretched higher than the left side, like a tilt of the body to the left.

Practice Exercise: Sway

Stand facing a mirror with the hip, ankle, and knee joints relaxed, and stretch the right side of the upper body higher than the left side. The head should remain with the tilt so that the spine and head are in the same line. Then stretch the left side of the upper body higher than the right side. Again, make sure the head remains in the same line as the body. Be aware of the feeling of the tilt in the body.

American Style Waltz

Waltz is the most classic of the ballroom dances. From being considered a scandalous dance in the 1800s to being the most popular dance that newlyweds use for their wedding dance, the waltz is the epitome of romance. It is characterized by a rising-and-falling motion as it travels around the floor. At a very high level, it is probably the most physically demanding of the ballroom dances. Advanced dancers develop a strong body swing action, which helps create the rise-and-fall movements. They also use more quick turning movements. But when the dance is done well, it looks soft with a floating quality. The music is written in 3/4 time, which means there are three beats to a bar of music. Everything is counted in groups of three—1, 2, 3.

As mentioned in chapter 5, several types of rise and fall are used in the waltz. The following is a list of all that are included in this chapter. Each step pattern has its own rise and fall depending on the positioning of the feet, which is noted in the description of the pattern.

- Figures that move in a forward direction and close on the third step—Start to rise at the end of 1, continue to rise on 2 and 3, and lower at the end of 3.

- Figures that move in a backward direction and close on the third step—Start to rise at the end of 1 through the body with no foot rise (which means your heel will remain on the floor as your body starts to rise), continue to rise on 2 and 3, and lower at the end of 3.

- Figures that move forward that have three steps and end with the feet apart—Start to rise at the end of 1, continue to rise on 2, up on 3, and lower at the end of 3.

- Figures that move backward that have three steps and end with the feet apart—Start to rise at the end of 1 through the body with no foot rise, continue to rise on 2, up on 3, and lower at the end of 3.

- Figures that do not have foot rise—Go down on 1, and slightly rise through the body on 2 and 3. The body lowers slightly at the end of 3. This rise and fall is expressed only in the body.

In the beginning of your learning, just learn where the feet are positioned and the amount of turn. When you understand that, add the rise and fall.

Most of the patterns in this chapter are basic social patterns. They are listed in order by the level of difficulty to enable you to get moving around the floor as quickly as possible. As you progress through the patterns, you will also find that elements from previous patterns reappear. So it's best to proceed through the step patterns in the order presented. The open left turn and the open right turn included at the end of this chapter are more intricate variations of the basic patterns. They include more movement, so a bigger dance floor is needed. To accomplish these patterns, the basic patterns and the general principles covered in chapters 4 and 5 must be understood. It's not recommended to combine the social and the intermediate patterns in waltz. Going back and forth between the two is confusing for both partners because sometimes the feet come together and sometimes they don't. However, sometimes it is necessary because of traffic on the floor. It will be easier when you have more experience; the man will have a better lead and the lady will be able to react to where his body goes and will be able to feel if his feet come together or not.

Refer to the explanations of posture and dance position in chapters 4 and 5, including promenade position and outside position. The details of footwork, foot position, and contrary body movement position (CBMP) are explained in chapter 4. The terms heel, ball, and toe are used to describe footwork. Contrary body movement (CBM) is detailed in chapter 5. Sway is explained in chapter 5 and is more evident in the waltz than in the other dances because of the strong rise-and-fall movements and the swinging action. But learn the basic foot positions before you try the rise and fall and sway. The alignments noted in the practice combinations are all written to explain the direction the man faces to begin the step pattern.

Waltz Step Patterns

Basic Social

Forward progressive basic

Left box turn—with no turn, turning one-quarter, turning three-eighths

Right box turn—with no turn, turning one-quarter, turning three-eighths

Hesitations—forward and backward and side

Single twinkle

Side by side progressive basic

Grapevine

Intermediate

Open left turn

Open right turn

FORWARD PROGRESSIVE BASIC

This step keeps you traveling down the line of dance and around the dance floor. It can be used to start the dance and any time forward progression is desired. It is also used to get on the correct foot to dance a specific pattern. In the practice exercises, it is noted as dancing half of the pattern, or dancing a left forward progressive basic or right forward progressive basic.

> See this technique demonstrated on the DVD

The pattern is usually done twice to keep the step in time with the music phrasing, but can be done as many times as needed to move as much as the dancers want to move. Once the step pattern is understood, a slight turn to the left (CBM) may be made when the left foot is going forward, and a slight turn to the right may be made when the right foot is going forward. This contrary body movement is the natural way that we walk, so it will create an ease of movement. It will also give the pattern a more flowing quality. Note that when the lady is moving backward, she will never have foot rise. Every backward moving step's footwork for the lady is toe, heel, even if there is a body rise.

Gentleman's Part

Step 1 (Beat 1)

- Facing line of dance (LOD), step forward with your left foot.
- The footwork is heel, toe.
- Start to rise at the end of this step.
- There is no sway.

Step 2 (Beat 2)

- Facing LOD, step side and slightly forward with the right foot.
- The footwork is toe.
- Continue to rise.
- Sway to the left.

Lady's Part

Step 1 (Beat 1)

- Backing LOD, step back with the right foot.
- The footwork is toe, heel.
- Start to rise through the body at the end of this step with no foot rise.
- There is no sway.

Step 2 (Beat 2)

- Backing LOD, step side and slightly back with the left foot.
- The footwork is toe.
- Continue to rise.
- Sway to the right.

(continued)

Forward Progressive Basic   *(continued)*

Gentleman's Part	**Lady's Part**

Step 3 (Beat 3)

- Facing LOD, close the left foot to the right foot.
- The footwork is toe, heel.
- Continue to rise and then lower to a flat foot at the end of the step.
- Sway to the left.

Step 4 (Beat 1)

- Facing LOD, step forward with the right foot.
- The footwork is heel, toe.
- Start to rise at the end of this step.
- There is no sway.

Step 5 (Beat 2)

- Facing LOD, step side and slightly forward with the left foot.
- The footwork is toe.
- Continue to rise.
- Sway to the right.

Step 6 (Beat 3)

- Facing LOD, close the right foot to the left foot.
- The footwork is toe, heel.
- Continue to rise and then lower to a flat foot at the end of the step.
- Sway to the right.

Step 3 (Beat 3)

- Backing LOD, close the right foot to the left foot.
- The footwork is toe, heel.
- Continue to rise and then lower to a flat foot at the end of the step.
- Sway to the right.

Step 4 (Beat 1)

- Backing LOD, step back with the left foot.
- The footwork is toe, heel.
- Start to rise through the body at the end of this step with no foot rise.
- There is no sway.

Step 5 (Beat 2)

- Backing LOD, step side and slightly back with the right foot.
- The footwork is toe.
- Continue to rise.
- Sway to the left.

Step 6 (Beat 3)

- Backing LOD, close the left foot to the right foot.
- The footwork is toe, heel.
- Continue to rise and then lower to a flat foot at the end of the step.
- Sway to the left.

LEFT BOX TURN

This pattern begins to use turn as an important element because forward progression and turn combine to give the waltz its characteristic flowing quality. First, it's best to learn the foot pattern with no turn. After you are certain of the steps and the foot pattern becomes natural, start to turn one-quarter of a turn over three steps. The ultimate goal is to turn the pattern three-eighths over three steps.

The left box turn with a quarter turn over three steps should only be used in a corner or in the center of the room because it cannot move along the line of dance. It will take two complete boxes, or 12 steps, to make a 360-degree turn, so you end where you start. To move down the floor, a left box turn must be turned three-eighths over three steps. In the beginning learning stages it will be much easier to turn only one-quarter over three steps, but as turning becomes more natural, it should evolve into a three-eighths turn so the dance can keep moving around the floor.

For the turning box steps, whoever is on the inside of the turn (or the person moving back) always turns the foot in the direction of the turn. That is why sometimes the alignments are written as pointing in a direction.

When looking at the alignments, remember that alignment means where the feet are facing, not necessarily where the body is facing. In some patterns, the direction of the feet and body might be different. Rise and fall and sway remain the same regardless of the amount of turn.

Left Box Turn With No Turn

> See this technique demonstrated on the DVD

Gentleman's Part

Step 1 (Beat 1)

- Facing LOD, step forward with the left foot (6.1*a*).
- The footwork is heel, toe.
- Start to rise at the end of this step.
- There is no sway.

Step 2 (Beat 2)

- Facing LOD, step side with the right foot.
- The footwork is toe.
- Continue to rise.
- Sway to the left.

Lady's Part

Step 1 (Beat 1)

- Backing LOD, step back with the right foot (6.1*a*).
- The footwork is toe, heel.
- Start to rise through the body at the end of this step with no foot rise.
- There is no sway.

Step 2 (Beat 2)

- Backing LOD, step side with the left foot.
- The footwork is toe.
- Continue to rise.
- Sway to the right.

(continued)

Left Box Turn With No Turn   *(continued)*

Gentleman's Part

Step 3 (Beat 3)

- Facing LOD, close the left foot to the right foot.
- The footwork is toe, heel.
- Continue to rise and then lower to a flat foot at the end of the step.
- Sway to the left.

Step 4 (Beat 1)

- Backing against LOD, step back with the right foot (6.1*b*).
- The footwork is toe, heel.
- Start to rise through the body at the end of this step with no foot rise.
- There is no sway.

Step 5 (Beat 2)

- Backing against LOD, step side with the left foot.
- The footwork is toe.
- Continue to rise.
- Sway to the right.

Step 6 (Beat 3)

- Backing against LOD, close the right foot to the left foot.
- The footwork is toe, heel.
- Continue to rise and then lower to a flat foot at the end of the step.
- Sway to the right.

Lady's Part

Step 3 (Beat 3)

- Backing LOD, close the right foot to the left foot.
- The footwork is toe, heel.
- Continue to rise and then lower to a flat foot at the end of the step.
- Sway to the right.

Step 4 (Beat 1)

- Facing against LOD, step forward with the left foot (6.1*b*).
- The footwork is heel, toe.
- Start to rise at the end of this step.
- There is no sway.

Step 5 (Beat 2)

- Facing against LOD, step side with the right foot.
- The footwork is toe.
- Continue to rise.
- Sway to the left.

Step 6 (Beat 3)

- Facing against LOD, close the left foot to the right foot.
- The footwork is toe, heel.
- Continue to rise and then lower to a flat foot at the end of the step.
- Sway to the left.

Figure 6.1 Left box turn with no turn: steps *(a)* 1 and *(b)* 4.

Left Box Turn: One-Quarter Over Three Steps

See this technique demonstrated on the DVD

Gentleman's Part

Step 1 (Beat 1)

- Facing LOD, step forward with the left foot.
- Start turning to the left.
- The footwork is heel, toe.
- Start to rise at the end of this step.
- There is no sway.

Step 2 (Beat 2)

- Backing wall, step side with the right foot.
- There is a quarter turn to the left between steps 1 and 2.
- The footwork is toe.
- Continue to rise.
- Sway to the left.

Lady's Part

Step 1 (Beat 1)

- Backing LOD, step back with the right foot.
- Start turning to the left.
- The footwork is toe, heel.
- Start to rise through the body at the end of this step with no foot rise.
- There is no sway.

Step 2 (Beat 2)

- Pointing wall, step side with the left foot.
- There is a quarter turn to the left between steps 1 and 2.
- The footwork is toe.
- Continue to rise.
- Sway to the right.

(continued)

Left Box Turn: One-Quarter Over Three Steps   *(continued)*

Gentleman's Part	**Lady's Part**

Step 3 (Beat 3)

- Backing wall, close the left foot to the right foot.
- The footwork is toe, heel.
- Continue to rise and then lower to a flat foot at the end of the step.
- Sway to the left.

Step 4 (Beat 1)

- Backing wall, step back with the right foot.
- Start turning to the left.
- The footwork is toe, heel.
- Start to rise through the body at the end of this step with no foot rise.
- There is no sway.

Step 5 (Beat 2)

- Pointing against LOD, step side with the left foot.
- There is a quarter turn to the left between steps 4 and 5.
- The footwork is toe.
- Continue to rise.
- Sway to the right.

Step 6 (Beat 3)

- Facing against LOD, close the right foot to the left foot.
- The footwork is toe, heel.
- Continue to rise and then lower to a flat foot at the end of the step.
- Sway to the right.

Step 3 (Beat 3)

- Facing wall, close the right foot to the left foot.
- The footwork is toe, heel.
- Continue to rise and then lower to a flat foot at the end of the step.
- Sway to the right.

Step 4 (Beat 1)

- Facing wall, step forward with the left foot.
- Start turning to the left.
- The footwork is heel, toe.
- Start to rise at the end of this step.
- There is no sway.

Step 5 (Beat 2)

- Backing against LOD, step side with the right foot.
- There is a quarter turn to the left between steps 4 and 5.
- The footwork is toe.
- Continue to rise.
- Sway to the left.

Step 6 (Beat 3)

- Backing against LOD, close the left foot to the right foot.
- The footwork is toe, heel.
- Continue to rise and then lower to a flat foot at the end of the step.
- Sway to the left.

Step 7 (Beat 1)

- Facing against LOD, step forward with the left foot.
- Start turning to the left.
- The footwork is heel, toe.
- Start to rise at the end of this step.
- There is no sway.

Step 8 (Beat 2)

- Backing center, step side with the right foot.
- There is a quarter turn to the left between steps 7 and 8.
- The footwork is toe.
- Continue to rise.
- Sway to the left.

Step 9 (Beat 3)

- Backing center, close the left foot to the right foot.
- The footwork is toe, heel.
- Continue to rise and then lower to a flat foot at the end of the step.
- Sway to the left.

Step 10 (Beat 1)

- Backing center, step back with the right foot.
- Start turning to the left.
- The footwork is toe, heel.
- Start to rise through the body at the end of this step with no foot rise.
- There is no sway.

Step 7 (Beat 1)

- Backing against LOD, step back with the right foot.
- Start turning to the left.
- The footwork is toe, heel.
- Start to rise through the body at the end of this step with no foot rise.
- There is no sway.

Step 8 (Beat 2)

- Pointing center, step side with the left foot.
- There is a quarter turn to the left between steps 7 and 8.
- The footwork is toe.
- Continue to rise.
- Sway to the right.

Step 9 (Beat 3)

- Facing center, close the right foot to the left foot.
- The footwork is toe, heel.
- Continue to rise and then lower to a flat foot at the end of the step.
- Sway to the right.

Step 10 (Beat 1)

- Facing center, step forward with the left foot.
- Start turning to the left.
- The footwork is heel, toe.
- Start to rise at the end of this step.
- There is no sway.

(continued)

Left Box Turn: One-Quarter Over Three Steps   *(continued)*

Gentleman's Part	Lady's Part

Step 11 (Beat 2)

- Pointing LOD, step side with the left foot.
- There is a quarter turn to the left between steps 10 and 11.
- The footwork is toe.
- Continue to rise.
- Sway to the right.

Step 11 (Beat 2)

- Backing LOD, step side with the right foot.
- There is a quarter turn to the left between steps 10 and 11.
- The footwork is toe.
- Continue to rise.
- Sway to the left.

Step 12 (Beat 3)

- Facing LOD, close the right foot to the left foot.
- The footwork is toe, heel.
- Continue to rise and then lower to a flat foot at the end of the step.
- Sway to the right.

Step 12 (Beat 3)

- Backing LOD, close the left foot to the right foot.
- The footwork is toe, heel.
- Continue to rise and then lower to a flat foot at the end of the step.
- Sway to the left.

Practice Combination

Two forward progressive basics—facing LOD

Two left box turns—turning one-quarter each time, which will turn all the way around to where you started

Two forward progressive basics—facing LOD

Left Box Turn: Three-Eighths Over Three Steps

See this technique demonstrated on the DVD

Gentleman's Part

Step 1 (Beat 1)

- Facing diagonal center (DC), step forward with the left foot.
- Start turning to the left.
- The footwork is heel, toe.
- Start to rise at the end of this step.
- There is no sway.

Step 2 (Beat 2)

- Backing diagonal wall (DW), step side with the right foot.
- There is a quarter turn to the left between steps 1 and 2.
- The footwork is toe.
- Continue to rise.
- Sway to the left.

Step 3 (Beat 3)

- Backing LOD, close the left foot to the right foot.
- There is an eighth turn to the left between steps 2 and 3.
- The footwork is toe, heel.
- Continue to rise and then lower to a flat foot at the end of the step.
- Sway to the left.

Step 4 (Beat 1)

- Backing LOD, step back with the right foot.
- Start turning to the left.
- The footwork is toe, heel.
- Start to rise through the body at the end of this step with no foot rise.
- There is no sway.

Lady's Part

Step 1 (Beat 1)

- Backing DC, step back with the right foot.
- Start turning to the left.
- The footwork is toe, heel.
- Start to rise through the body at the end of this step with no foot rise.
- There is no sway.

Step 2 (Beat 2)

- Pointing LOD, step side with the left foot.
- There is a three-eighths turn to the left between steps 1 and 2.
- The footwork is toe.
- Continue to rise.
- Sway to the right.

Step 3 (Beat 3)

- Facing LOD, close the right foot to the left foot.
- The footwork is toe, heel.
- Continue to rise and then lower to a flat foot at the end of the step.
- Sway to the right.

Step 4 (Beat 1)

- Facing LOD, step forward with the left foot.
- Start turning to the left.
- The footwork is heel, toe.
- Start to rise at the end of this step.
- There is no sway.

(continued)

Left Box Turn: Three-Eighths Over Three Steps   *(continued)*

Gentleman's Part

Step 5 (Beat 2)

- Pointing DW, step side with the left foot.
- There is a three-eighths turn to the left between steps 4 and 5.
- The footwork is toe.
- Continue to rise.
- Sway to the right.

Step 6 (Beat 3)

- Facing DW, close the right foot to the left foot.
- The footwork is toe, heel.
- Continue to rise and then lower to a flat foot at the end of the step.
- Sway to the right.

Lady's Part

Step 5 (Beat 2)

- Backing wall, step side with the right foot.
- There is a quarter turn to the left between steps 4 and 5.
- The footwork is toe.
- Continue to rise.
- Sway to the left.

Step 6 (Beat 3)

- Backing DW, close the left foot to the right foot.
- There is an eighth turn to the left between steps 5 and 6.
- The footwork is toe, heel.
- Continue to rise and then lower to a flat foot at the end of the step.
- Sway to the left.

RIGHT BOX TURN

This pattern is basically the same as the left box turn, but it turns to the right. The process of learning the right box turn is the same as for the left box turn. In the beginning, learn the right box with no turn. Then turn the right box turn a quarter of a turn over three steps. That will take two complete boxes, or 12 steps, to finish in the same direction that the box was started. When turning becomes more natural, turn the box three-eighths of a turn over three steps.

Right Box Turn With No Turn

See this technique demonstrated on the DVD

Gentleman's Part

Step 1 (Beat 1)

- Facing LOD, step forward with the right foot (6.2*a*).
- The footwork is heel, toe.
- Start to rise at the end of this step.
- There is no sway.

Step 2 (Beat 2)

- Facing LOD, step side with the left foot.
- The footwork is toe.
- Continue to rise.
- Sway to the right.

Step 3 (Beat 3)

- Facing LOD, close the right foot to the left foot.
- The footwork is toe, heel.
- Continue to rise and then lower to a flat foot at the end of the step.
- Sway to the right.

Step 4 (Beat 1)

- Backing against LOD, step back with the left foot (6.2*b*).
- The footwork is toe, heel.
- Start to rise through the body at the end of this step with no foot rise.
- There is no sway.

Lady's Part

Step 1 (Beat 1)

- Backing LOD, step back with the left foot (6.2*a*).
- The footwork is toe, heel.
- Start to rise through the body at the end of this step with no foot rise.
- There is no sway.

Step 2 (Beat 2)

- Backing LOD, step side with the right foot.
- The footwork is toe.
- Continue to rise.
- Sway to the left.

Step 3 (Beat 3)

- Backing LOD, close the left foot to the right foot.
- The footwork is toe, heel.
- Continue to rise and then lower to a flat foot at the end of the step.
- Sway to the left.

Step 4 (Beat 1)

- Facing against LOD, step forward with the right foot (6.2*b*).
- The footwork is heel, toe.
- Start to rise at the end of this step.
- There is no sway.

(continued)

Right Box Turn With No Turn　　*(continued)*

Gentleman's Part

Step 5 (Beat 2)

- Backing against LOD, step side with the right foot.
- The footwork is toe.
- Continue to rise.
- Sway to the left.

Step 6 (Beat 3)

- Backing against LOD, close the left foot to the right foot.
- The footwork is toe, heel.
- Continue to rise and then lower to a flat foot at the end of the step.
- Sway to the left.

Lady's Part

Step 5 (Beat 2)

- Facing against LOD, step side with the left foot.
- The footwork is toe.
- Continue to rise.
- Sway to the right.

Step 6 (Beat 3)

- Facing against LOD, close the right foot to the left foot.
- The footwork is toe, heel.
- Continue to rise and then lower to a flat foot at the end of the step.
- Sway to the right.

Figure 6.2　Right box turn with no turn: steps *(a)* 1 and *(b)* 4.

Right Box Turn: One-Quarter Over Three Steps

See this technique demonstrated on the DVD

Gentleman's Part

Step 1 (Beat 1)

- Facing LOD, step forward with the right foot.
- Start turning to the right.
- The footwork is heel, toe.
- Start to rise at the end of this step.
- There is no sway.

Step 2 (Beat 2)

- Backing center, step side with the left foot.
- There is a quarter turn to the right between steps 1 and 2.
- The footwork is toe.
- Continue to rise.
- Sway to the right.

Step 3 (Beat 3)

- Backing center, close the right foot to the left foot.
- The footwork is toe, heel.
- Continue to rise and then lower to a flat foot at the end of the step.
- Sway to the right.

Step 4 (Beat 1)

- Backing center, step back with the left foot.
- Start turning to the right.
- The footwork is toe, heel.
- Start to rise through the body at the end of this step with no foot rise.
- There is no sway.

Lady's Part

Step 1 (Beat 1)

- Backing LOD, step back with the left foot.
- Start turning to the right.
- The footwork is toe, heel.
- Start to rise through the body at the end of this step with no foot rise.
- There is no sway.

Step 2 (Beat 2)

- Facing center, step side with the right foot.
- There is a quarter turn to the right between steps 1 and 2.
- The footwork is toe.
- Continue to rise.
- Sway to the left.

Step 3 (Beat 3)

- Facing center, close the left foot to the right foot.
- The footwork is toe, heel.
- Continue to rise and then lower to a flat foot at the end of the step.
- Sway to the left.

Step 4 (Beat 1)

- Facing center, step forward with the right foot.
- Start turning to the right.
- The footwork is heel, toe.
- Start to rise at the end of this step.
- There is no sway.

(continued)

Right Box Turn: One-Quarter Over Three Steps   *(continued)*

Gentleman's Part

Step 5 (Beat 2)

- Pointing against LOD, step side with the right foot.
- There is a quarter turn to the right between steps 4 and 5.
- The footwork is toe.
- Continue to rise.
- Sway to the left.

Step 6 (Beat 3)

- Facing against LOD, close the left foot to the right foot.
- The footwork is toe, heel.
- Continue to rise and then lower to a flat foot at the end of the step.
- Sway to the left.

Step 7 (Beat 1)

- Facing against LOD, step forward with the right foot.
- Start turning to the right.
- The footwork is heel, toe.
- Start to rise at the end of this step.
- There is no sway.

Step 8 (Beat 2)

- Backing wall, step side with the left foot.
- There is a quarter turn to the right between steps 7 and 8.
- The footwork is toe.
- Continue to rise.
- Sway to the right.

Lady's Part

Step 5 (Beat 2)

- Backing against LOD, step side with the left foot.
- There is a quarter turn to the right between steps 4 and 5.
- The footwork is toe.
- Continue to rise.
- Sway to the right.

Step 6 (Beat 3)

- Backing against LOD, close the right foot to the left foot.
- The footwork is toe, heel.
- Continue to rise and then lower to a flat foot at the end of the step.
- Sway to the right.

Step 7 (Beat 1)

- Backing against LOD, step back with the left foot.
- Start turning to the right.
- The footwork is toe, heel.
- Start to rise through the body at the end of this step with no foot rise.
- There is no sway.

Step 8 (Beat 2)

- Facing wall, step side with the right foot.
- There is a quarter turn to the right between steps 7 and 8
- The footwork is toe.
- Continue to rise.
- Sway to the left.

Step 9 (Beat 3)

- Backing wall, close the right foot to the left foot.
- The footwork is toe, heel.
- Continue to rise and then lower to a flat foot at the end of the step.
- Sway to the right.

Step 10 (Beat 1)

- Backing wall, step back with the left foot.
- Start turning to the right.
- The footwork is toe, heel.
- Start to rise through the body at the end of this step with no foot rise.
- There is no sway.

Step 11 (Beat 2)

- Pointing LOD, step side with the right foot.
- There is a quarter turn to the right between steps 10 and 11.
- The footwork is toe.
- Continue to rise.
- Sway to the left.

Step 12 (Beat 3)

- Facing LOD, close the left foot to the right foot.
- The footwork is toe, heel.
- Continue to rise and then lower to a flat foot at the end of the step.
- Sway to the left.

Step 9 (Beat 3)

- Facing wall, close the left foot to the right foot.
- The footwork is toe, heel.
- Continue to rise and then lower to a flat foot at the end of the step.
- Sway to the left.

Step 10 (Beat 1)

- Facing wall, step forward with the right foot.
- Start turning to the right.
- The footwork is heel, toe.
- Start to rise at the end of this step.
- There is no sway.

Step 11 (Beat 2)

- Backing LOD, step side with the left foot.
- There is a quarter turn to the right between steps 10 and 11.
- The footwork is toe.
- Continue to rise.
- Sway to the right.

Step 12 (Beat 3)

- Backing LOD, close the right foot to the left foot.
- The footwork is toe, heel.
- Continue to rise and then lower to a flat foot at the end of the step.
- Sway to the right.

Practice Combination

One and a half forward progressive basics—facing LOD

Two right box turns—turning a quarter each time, which will turn all the way around to where you started

One and a half forward progressive basics—starting with right foot facing LOD

See this technique demonstrated on the DVD

Right Box Turn: Three-Eighths Over Three Steps

Gentleman's Part

Step 1 (Beat 1)

- Facing DW, step forward with the right foot.
- Start turning to the right.
- The footwork is heel, toe.
- Start to rise at the end of this step.
- There is no sway.

Step 2 (Beat 2)

- Backing DC, step side with the left foot.
- There is a quarter turn to the right between steps 1 and 2.
- The footwork is toe.
- Continue to rise.
- Sway to the right.

Step 3 (Beat 3)

- Backing LOD, close the right foot to the left foot.
- There is an eighth turn to the right between steps 2 and 3.
- The footwork is toe, heel.
- Continue to rise and then lower to a flat foot at the end of the step.
- Sway to the right.

Lady's Part

Step 1 (Beat 1)

- Backing DW, step back with the left foot.
- Start turning to the right.
- The footwork is toe, heel.
- Start to rise through the body at the end of this step with no foot rise.
- There is no sway.

Step 2 (Beat 2)

- Pointing LOD, step side with the right foot.
- There is a three-eighths turn to the right between steps 1 and 2.
- The footwork is toe.
- Continue to rise.
- Sway to the left.

Step 3 (Beat 3)

- Facing LOD, close the left foot to the right foot.
- The footwork is toe, heel.
- Continue to rise and then lower to a flat foot at the end of the step.
- Sway to the left.

Step 4 (Beat 1)

- Backing LOD, step back with the left foot.
- Start turning to the right.
- The footwork is toe, heel.
- Start to rise through the body at the end of this step with no foot rise.
- There is no sway.

Step 5 (Beat 2)

- Pointing DC, step side with the right foot.
- There is a three-eighths turn to the right between steps 4 and 5.
- The footwork is toe.
- Continue to rise.
- Sway to the left.

Step 6 (Beat 3)

- Facing DC, close the left foot to the right foot.
- The footwork is toe, heel.
- Continue to rise and then lower to a flat foot at the end of the step.
- Sway to the left.

Step 4 (Beat 1)

- Facing LOD, step forward with the right foot.
- Start turning to the right.
- The footwork is heel, toe.
- Start to rise at the end of this step.
- There is no sway.

Step 5 (Beat 2)

- Backing center, step side with the left foot.
- There is a quarter turn to the right between steps 4 and 5.
- The footwork is toe.
- Continue to rise.
- Sway to the right.

Step 6 (Beat 3)

- Backing DC, close the right foot to the left foot.
- There is an eighth turn to the right between steps 5 and 6.
- The footwork is toe, heel.
- Continue to rise and then lower to a flat foot at the end of the step.
- Sway to the right.

Left and Right Box Turn Combination

To progress down the line of dance, the left and right boxes turning three-eighths of a turn are combined with half of a forward progressive basic between the boxes. Dancing just left boxes or just right boxes would not progress around the room because of the amount of turn that is possible to achieve. To dance the two patterns together, start with the left box turn facing diagonal center and ending diagonal wall. Then perform the left forward progressive basic with no turn. Next, dance the right box turn facing DW and ending DC. And finish with a right forward progressive basic with no turn.

See this technique demonstrated on the DVD

This combination can be continued as many times as desired. In a corner you can turn the right and left boxes any amount, up to three-eighths of a turn over three steps, until you are facing the desired alignment.

Practice Combination

Left box turn—turning three-eighths, start facing DC

Left forward progressive basic—facing DW

Right box turn—turning three-eighths, start facing DW, end facing DC

Right forward progressive basic—facing DC

HESITATIONS

The name of this step pattern, hesitations, perfectly explains its purpose. Hesitations keep you dancing in time to the music even if you have to stop briefly to keep from running into another couple. This is one of the evasive steps previously mentioned. Hesitations should be used only when there is a traffic jam in order to get out of trouble. (How the man conveys what he wants to do was explained in chapter 5.) These patterns may be used in any alignment. Because there is no turn, they finish the same way they start.

The hesitations are danced with a slight body rise but no foot rise. Keep ankle, knee, and hip joints relaxed so you can move easily from foot to foot. Keep pressure on the closing foot for better balance, but do not put all the weight on it. There is no sway in the hesitations.

See this technique
demonstrated on
the DVD

Forward and Backward Hesitations

Gentleman's Part

Step 1 (Beat 1)

- Facing LOD, step forward with the left foot.
- Footwork is heel.

Step 2 (Beat 2)

- Facing LOD, close the right foot to the left foot with no weight.
- Footwork is ball.

Lady's Part

Step 1 (Beat 1)

- Backing LOD, step back with the right foot.
- Footwork is toe, heel.

Step 2 (Beat 2)

- Backing LOD, close the left foot to the right foot with no weight.
- Footwork is ball.

Step 3 (Beat 3)

- Facing LOD, hold that position without changing weight.
- Footwork is pressure on ball of right foot.

Step 4 (Beat 1)

- Backing against LOD, step back with the right foot.
- Footwork is toe, heel.

Step 5 (Beat 2)

- Backing against LOD, close the left foot to the right foot with no weight.
- Footwork is ball.

Step 6 (Beat 3)

- Backing against LOD, hold that position without changing weight.
- Footwork is pressure on ball of left foot.

Step 3 (Beat 3)

- Backing LOD, hold that position without changing weight.
- Footwork is pressure on ball of left foot.

Step 4 (Beat 1)

- Facing against LOD, step forward with the left foot.
- Footwork is heel.

Step 5 (Beat 2)

- Facing against LOD, close the right foot to the left foot with no weight.
- Footwork is ball.

Step 6 (Beat 3)

- Facing against LOD, hold that position without changing weight.
- Footwork is pressure on ball of right foot.

Side Hesitations

See this technique demonstrated on the DVD

Gentleman's Part

Step 1 (Beat 1)

- Facing LOD, step side with the left foot.
- Footwork is toe, heel.

Step 2 (Beat 2)

- Facing LOD, close the right foot to the left foot with no weight.
- Footwork is ball.

Lady's Part

Step 1 (Beat 1)

- Backing LOD, step side with the right foot.
- Footwork is toe, heel.

Step 2 (Beat 2)

- Backing LOD, close the left foot to the right foot with no weight.
- Footwork is ball.

(continued)

Side Hesitations   *(continued)*

Gentleman's Part	**Lady's Part**

Step 3 (Beat 3)

- Facing LOD, hold that position without changing weight.
- Footwork is pressure on ball of right foot.

Step 4 (Beat 1)

- Facing LOD, step side with the right foot.
- Footwork is toe, heel.

Step 5 (Beat 2)

- Facing LOD, close the left foot to the right foot with no weight.
- Footwork is ball.

Step 6 (Beat 3)

- Facing LOD, hold that position without changing weight.
- Footwork is pressure on ball of left foot.

Step 3 (Beat 3)

- Backing LOD, hold that position without changing weight.
- Footwork is pressure on ball of left foot

Step 4 (Beat 1)

- Backing LOD, step side with the left foot.
- Footwork is toe, heel.

Step 5 (Beat 2)

- Backing LOD, close the right foot to the left foot with no weight.
- Footwork is ball.

Step 6 (Beat 3)

- Backing LOD, hold that position without changing weight.
- Footwork is pressure on ball of right foot.

Practice Combination

Left box turn—turning three-eighths and end facing DW

Forward and backward hesitations—no turn

Left forward progressive basic—facing DW

Right box turn—turning three-eighths and end facing DC

Right forward progressive basic—facing DC

Side hesitations—facing DC

SINGLE TWINKLE

The single twinkle is a pattern that begins and ends many intermediate and advanced patterns. It will take you from closed to promenade position and then back to closed position. But the pattern may be used on its own to move slightly down the floor or to change the direction of the dance.

Two variations will show the pattern ending in two different room alignments, which means it will open two different directions. Rise and fall, sway, posture, and dance position are the same for all variations of the twinkle.

The twinkle can be opened to promenade to the left or right, depending on where you want to move on the floor. When opening to promenade to the right, there is a slight upper-body turn to the right between steps 1 and 2 for the gentleman to tell the lady to turn her feet to the right. When opening to the left, there is a slight foot turn to the left for the gentleman to move into promenade position. (For more information, refer to Turning to Promenade Position in chapter 5.) Promenade position is always the same at the end regardless of whether it opens to the right or left.

Single Twinkle: Opening to Promenade to the Right

> See this technique demonstrated on the DVD

Gentleman's Part

Step 1 (Beat 1)

- Facing DW, step forward with the left foot.
- There is no turn of the feet in this figure.
- The footwork is heel, toe.
- Start to rise at the end of this step.

Step 2 (Beat 2)

- Facing DW, step side and slightly forward with the right foot.
- There is a slight body turn to the right.
- The footwork is toe.
- Continue to rise.

Lady's Part

Step 1 (Beat 1)

- Backing DW, step back with the right foot.
- The footwork is toe, heel.
- Start to rise through the body at the end of this step with no foot rise.

Step 2 (Beat 2)

- Pointing DC, step diagonally back with the left foot.
- There is a quarter turn to the right between steps 1 and 2.
- The footwork is toe.
- Continue to rise.

(continued)

Single Twinkle: Opening to Promenade to the Right   *(continued)*

Gentleman's Part

Step 3 (Beat 3)

- Facing DW, close the left foot to the right foot (6.3*a*, *b*).
- The footwork is toe, heel.
- Continue to rise and then lower to a flat foot at the end of the step.

Step 4 (Beat 1)

- Facing DW and moving along LOD, step forward and across in promenade position with the right foot (6.3*c*, *d*).
- The footwork is heel, toe.
- Start to rise at the end of the step.

Step 5 (Beat 2)

- Facing DW, step side and slightly forward with the left foot.
- The footwork is toe.
- Continue to rise.

Step 6 (Beat 3)

- Facing DW, close the right foot to the left foot.
- The footwork is toe, heel.
- Continue to rise and then lower at the end of the step.

Lady's Part

Step 3 (Beat 3)

- Facing DC, close the right foot to the left foot in promenade position (6.3*a*, *b*).
- The footwork is toe, heel.
- Continue to rise and then lower to a flat foot at the end of the step.

Step 4 (Beat 1)

- Facing DC and moving along LOD, step forward and across with the left foot in promenade position (6.3*c*, *d*).
- The footwork is heel, toe.
- Start to rise at the end of this step.

Step 5 (Beat 2)

- Backing wall, step side with the right foot.
- There is an eighth turn to the left between steps 4 and 5.
- The footwork is toe.
- Continue to rise.

Step 6 (Beat 3)

- Backing DW, close the left foot to the right foot.
- There is an eighth turn to the left between steps 5 and 6.
- The footwork is toe, heel.
- Continue to rise and then lower to a flat foot at the end of the step.

Figure 6.3 Single twinkle opening to promenade: steps *(a, b)* 3 and *(c, d)* 4.

Practice Combination

Left box turn—turning three-eighths, end facing DW

Single twinkle opening to the right—start and end facing DW

Left forward progressive basic—facing DW

Right box turn—turning three-eighths, end facing DC

Right forward progressive basic—facing DC

See this technique demonstrated on the DVD

Single Twinkle: Opening to Promenade to the Left

Gentleman's Part

Step 1 (Beat 1)

- Facing DW, step forward with the left foot.
- The footwork is heel, toe.
- Start to rise at the end of this step.

Step 2 (Beat 2)

- Facing LOD, step diagonally forward with the right foot.
- There is an eighth turn to the left between steps 1 and 2.
- The footwork is toe.
- Continue to rise.

Step 3 (Beat 3)

- Facing DC, close the left foot to the right foot in promenade position.
- There is an eighth turn to the left between steps 2 and 3.
- The footwork is toe, heel.
- Continue to rise and then lower to a flat foot at the end of the step.

Step 4 (Beat 1)

- Facing DC and moving toward center, step forward and across in promenade position with the right foot.
- The footwork is heel, toe.
- Start to rise at the end of the step.

Lady's Part

Step 1 (Beat 1)

- Backing DW, step back with the right foot.
- The footwork is toe, heel.
- Start to rise through the body at the end of this step with no foot rise.

Step 2 (Beat 2)

- Backing DW, step back with the left foot.
- There is no foot turn.
- The footwork is toe.
- Continue to rise.

Step 3 (Beat 3)

- Facing DC against LOD, close the right foot to the left foot in promenade position.
- The footwork is toe, heel.
- Continue to rise and then lower to a flat foot at the end of the step.

Step 4 (Beat 1)

- Facing DC against LOD and moving to center, step forward and across with the left foot in promenade position.
- The footwork is heel, toe.
- Start to rise at the end of this step.

Step 5 (Beat 2)

- Facing DC, step side and slightly forward with the left foot.
- The footwork is toe.
- Continue to rise.

Step 6 (Beat 3)

- Facing DC, close the right foot to the left foot.
- The footwork is toe, heel.
- Continue to rise and then lower at the end of the step.

Step 5 (Beat 2)

- Backing LOD, step side with the right foot.
- There is an eighth turn to the left between steps 4 and 5.
- The footwork is toe.
- Continue to rise.

Step 6 (Beat 3)

- Backing DC, close the left foot to the right foot.
- There is an eighth turn to the left between steps 5 and 6.
- The footwork is toe, heel.
- Continue to rise and then lower to a flat foot at the end of the step.

Practice Combination

Left box turn—turning three-eighths, end facing DW

Single twinkle opening to the left—start facing DW and end facing DC

Left box turn—turning three-eighths

SIDE BY SIDE PROGRESSIVE BASIC

This pattern keeps moving along the line of dance. It is a nice pattern for getting out of closed dance position for a few measures, and it looks showy. It can only be used when there is ample space to move freely because the partners are not in closed position but move away from each other in a side-by-side position, and then back together again.

> See this technique demonstrated on the DVD

East Dunbartonshire Council

Gentleman's Part

Step 1 (Beat 1)

- Facing center, step forward with the left foot.
- The footwork is heel, toe.
- Start to rise at the end of this step.
- There is no sway.

Step 2 (Beat 2)

- Facing center, step side with the right foot.
- The footwork is toe.
- Continue to rise.
- Sway to the left.

Step 3 (Beat 3)

- Facing center, close the left foot to the right foot.
- The footwork is toe, heel.
- Continue to rise and then lower to a flat foot at the end of the step.
- Sway to the left.

Step 4 (Beat 1)

- Facing LOD, step forward with the right foot (6.4a).
- There is a quarter turn to the right.
- The footwork is heel, toe.
- Start to rise at the end of this step.
- There is no sway.

Lady's Part

Step 1 (Beat 1)

- Backing center, step back with the right foot.
- The footwork is toe, heel.
- Start to rise through the body at the end of this step with no foot rise.
- There is no sway.

Step 2 (Beat 2)

- Backing center, step side with the left foot.
- The footwork is toe.
- Continue to rise.
- Sway to the right.

Step 3 (Beat 3)

- Backing center, close the left foot to the right foot.
- The footwork is toe, heel.
- Continue to rise and then lower to a flat foot at the end of the step.
- Sway to the right.

Step 4 (Beat 1)

- Facing LOD, step forward with the left foot (6.4a).
- There is a quarter turn to the left.
- The footwork is heel, toe.
- Start to rise at the end of this step.
- There is no sway.

Step 5 (Beat 2)

- Facing DW, step side with the left foot (6.4*b*).
- There is an eighth turn to the right between steps 4 and 5.
- The footwork is toe.
- Continue to rise.
- Sway to the right.

Step 6 (Beat 3)

- Facing DW, close the right foot to the left foot (6.4*c*).
- The footwork is toe, heel.
- Continue to rise and then lower to a flat foot at the end of the step.
- Sway to the right.

Step 7 (Beat 1)

- Facing LOD, step forward with the left foot (6.4*d*).
- There is an eighth turn to the left between steps 6 and 7.
- The footwork is heel, toe.
- Start to rise at the end of this step.
- There is no sway.

Step 8 (Beat 2)

- Facing center, step side with the right foot (6.4*e*).
- There is a quarter turn to the left between steps 7 and 8.
- The footwork is toe.
- Continue to rise.
- Sway to the left.

Step 5 (Beat 2)

- Facing DC, step side with the right foot (6.4*b*).
- There is an eighth turn to the left between steps 4 and 5.
- The footwork is toe.
- Continue to rise.
- Sway to the left.

Step 6 (Beat 3)

- Facing DC, close the right foot to the left foot (6.4*c*).
- The footwork is toe, heel.
- Continue to rise and then lower to a flat foot at the end of the step.
- Sway to the left.

Step 7 (Beat 1)

- Facing LOD, step forward with the right foot (6.4*d*).
- There is an eighth turn to the right between steps 6 and 7.
- The footwork is heel, toe.
- Start to rise at the end of this step.
- There is no sway.

Step 8 (Beat 2)

- Facing wall, step side with the left foot (6.4*e*).
- There is a quarter turn to the right between steps 7 and 8.
- The footwork is toe.
- Continue to rise.
- Sway to the right.

(continued)

Side by Side Progressive Basic *(continued)*

Gentleman's Part	Lady's Part

Gentleman's Part

Step 9 (Beat 3)
- Facing center, close the left foot to the right foot (6.4f).
- The footwork is toe, heel.
- Continue to rise and then lower to a flat foot at the end of the step.
- Sway to the left.

Step 10 (Beat 1)
- Backing wall, step back with the right foot.
- The footwork is toe, heel.
- Start to rise through the body at the end of this step with no foot rise.
- There is no sway.

Step 11 (Beat 2)
- Backing wall, step side with the left foot.
- The footwork is toe.
- Continue to rise.
- Sway to the right.

Step 12 (Beat 3)
- Backing wall, close the right foot to the left foot.
- The footwork is toe, heel.
- Continue to rise and then lower to a flat foot at the end of the step.
- Sway to the right.

Lady's Part

Step 9 (Beat 3)
- Facing wall, close the right foot to the left foot (6.4f).
- The footwork is toe, heel.
- Continue to rise and then lower to a flat foot at the end of the step.
- Sway to the right.

Step 10 (Beat 1)
- Facing wall, step forward with the left foot.
- The footwork is heel, toe.
- Start to rise at the end of this step.
- There is no sway.

Step 11 (Beat 2)
- Facing wall, step side with the right foot.
- The footwork is toe.
- Continue to rise.
- Sway to the left.

Step 12 (Beat 3)
- Facing wall, close the left foot to the right foot.
- The footwork is toe, heel.
- Continue to rise and then lower to a flat foot at the end of the step.
- Sway to the left.

Figure 6.4 Side by side progressive basic: steps *(a)* 4, *(b)* 5, *(c)* 6, *(d)* 7, *(e)* 8, and *(f)* 9.

Practice Combination

Left box turn—turning a quarter on the first half and an eighth on the second half, start facing DW, end facing center

Side by side progressive basic

Left box turn—turning a quarter on the first half and three-eighths on the second half, end facing DW

GRAPEVINE

See this technique demonstrated on the DVD

This pattern is a nice moving step and is a stepping-stone to more advanced patterns. The grapevine introduces new elements that were not a part of the patterns learned thus far. It is the first time that a count of three does not end with the feet together and the first time there are steps in outside position (step 2 of the gentleman's part and step 4 of the lady's part). You need ample space to dance this pattern correctly. It may be used anywhere there is room.

Gentleman's Part

Step 1 (Beat 1)

- Facing DW, step forward with the left foot (6.5*a*).
- The footwork is heel, toe.
- Start to rise at the end of this step.
- There is no sway.

Step 2 (Beat 2)

- Facing DW, step forward with the right foot in outside position (6.5*b*).
- Start to turn right.
- The footwork is toe.
- Continue to rise.
- There is no sway.

Lady's Part

Step 1 (Beat 1)

- Backing DW, step back with the right foot (6.5*a*).
- The footwork is toe, heel.
- Start to rise through the body at the end of this step with no foot rise.
- There is no sway.

Step 2 (Beat 2)

- Backing DW, step back with the left foot (6.5*b*).
- Start to turn to the right.
- The footwork is toe.
- Continue to rise.
- There is no sway.

Step 3 (Beat 3)

- Backing DC, step side and slightly back with the left foot (6.5c).
- There is a quarter turn to the right between steps 2 and 3.
- The footwork is toe, heel.
- Up and then lower to a flat foot at the end of this step.

Step 4 (Beat 1)

- Backing DC, step back with the right foot (6.5d).
- Start to turn left.
- The footwork is toe, heel.
- Start to rise through the body at the end of this step with no foot rise.
- There is no sway.

Step 5 (Beat 2)

- Pointing DW, step side with the left foot.
- There is a quarter turn to the left between steps 4 and 5.
- The footwork is toe.
- Continue to rise.
- Sway to the right.

Step 6 (Beat 3)

- Facing DW, close the right foot to the left foot.
- The footwork is toe, heel.
- Continue to rise and then lower to a flat foot at the end of the step.
- Sway to the right.

Step 3 (Beat 3)

- Pointing DC, step side and slightly forward with the right foot (6.5c).
- There is a quarter turn to the right between steps 2 and 3.
- The footwork is toe, heel.
- Up and then lower to a flat foot at the end of this step.
- There is no sway.

Step 4 (Beat 1)

- Facing DC, step forward with the left foot in outside position on the partner's left side (6.5d).
- Start to turn left.
- The footwork is heel, toe.
- Start to rise at the end of this step.
- There is no sway.

Step 5 (Beat 2)

- Backing wall, step side with the right foot.
- There is an eighth turn to the left between steps 4 and 5.
- The footwork is toe.
- Continue to rise.
- Sway to the left.

Step 6 (Beat 3)

- Backing DW, close the left foot to the right foot.
- There is an eighth turn to the left between steps 5 and 6.
- The footwork is toe, heel.
- Continue to rise and then lower to a flat foot at the end of the step.
- Sway to the left.

(continued)

Grapevine   *(continued)*

Figure 6.5   Grapevine: steps *(a)* 1, *(b)* 2, *(c)* 3, and *(d)* 4.

Practice Combination

Left box turn—turning three-eighths, start DC and end DW
Grapevine—start DW and end DW

OPEN LEFT TURN

The open left turn is an intermediate-level step pattern. The difference between the left box turn and the open left turn is that instead of bringing the feet together at the end of the pattern as in the left box turn, the feet are in open position at the end of the open left turn. Open foot position means that one foot moves in front of or passes the other foot. This pattern should only be used when there is a large dance floor and when both dancers in the partnership have a good understanding of the basic elements of dancing and partnering, such as amount of turn, alignments, and dance position. It is easily combined with the open right turn to progress around the floor. Note that in both the gentleman's and lady's parts, there is a right outside position on steps 3 and 6.

> See this technique demonstrated on the DVD

Gentleman's Part

Step 1 (Beat 1)

- Facing DC, step forward with the left foot.
- Start turning to the left.
- The footwork is heel, toe.
- Start to rise at the end of this step.
- There is no sway.

Step 2 (Beat 2)

- Backing DW, step side with the right foot.
- There is a quarter turn to the left between steps 1 and 2.
- The footwork is toe.
- Continue to rise.
- Sway to the left.

Lady's Part

Step 1 (Beat 1)

- Backing DC, step back with the right foot.
- Start turning to the left.
- The footwork is toe, heel.
- Start to rise through the body at the end of this step with no foot rise.
- There is no sway.

Step 2 (Beat 2)

- Pointing LOD, step side and slightly forward with the left foot.
- There is a three-eighths turn to the left between steps 1 and 2.
- The footwork is toe.
- Continue to rise.
- Sway to the right.

(continued)

Open Left Turn *(continued)*

Gentleman's Part	**Lady's Part**

Step 3 (Beat 3)

- Backing LOD, step back with the left foot in CBMP (6.6*a*).
- There is an eighth turn to the left between steps 2 and 3.
- The footwork is toe, heel.
- Up and then lower to a flat foot at the end of the step.
- Sway to the left.

Step 4 (Beat 1)

- Backing LOD, step back with the right foot.
- Start turning to the left.
- The footwork is toe, heel.
- Start to rise through the body at the end of this step with no foot rise.
- There is no sway.

Step 5 (Beat 2)

- Pointing DW, step side and slightly forward with the left foot.
- There is a three-eighths turn to the left between steps 4 and 5.
- The footwork is toe.
- Continue to rise.
- Sway to the right.

Step 6 (Beat 3)

- Facing DW, step forward with the right foot in CBMP and outside position (6.6*b*).
- The footwork is toe, heel.
- Up and then lower to a flat foot at the end of the step.
- Sway to the right.

Step 3 (Beat 3)

- Facing LOD, step forward with the right foot in outside position and CBMP (6.6*a*).
- The footwork is toe, heel.
- Up and then lower to a flat foot at the end of the step.
- Sway to the right.

Step 4 (Beat 1)

- Facing LOD, step forward with the left foot.
- Start turning to the left.
- The footwork is heel, toe.
- Start to rise at the end of this step.
- There is no sway.

Step 5 (Beat 2)

- Backing wall, step side with the right foot.
- There is a quarter turn to the left between steps 4 and 5.
- The footwork is toe, heel.
- Continue to rise.
- Sway to the left.

Step 6 (Beat 3)

- Backing DW, step back with the left foot in CBMP (6.6*b*).
- There is an eighth turn to the left between steps 5 and 6.
- The footwork is toe, heel.
- Up and then lower to a flat foot at the end of the step.
- Sway to the left.

Figure 6.6   Open left turn: steps (a) 3 and (b) 6.

OPEN RIGHT TURN

The open right turn is also an intermediate-level step pattern. The name sounds similar to the right box turn, but there is not much similarity, except that the pattern turns to the right. It is used in combination with the open left turn to move the dancers around the floor comfortably. As with the open left turn, both partners need to have a very good understanding of basic dance skills to be able to accomplish this pattern. This pattern also introduces a heel turn for the man, which is an advanced movement. As the name implies, there is an actual turn on the man's left heel. When you are first learning the step, it is acceptable to just bring your feet together instead of dancing a heel turn. After you have practiced it and are comfortable with the movement, add that footwork to the step pattern.

See this technique demonstrated on the DVD

There is a slight upper-body turn to the right on step 2 for the gentleman to tell the lady to turn her feet to the right. Refer to Turning to Promenade Position in chapter 5. Note that for both the gentleman's and lady's parts, there is a right outside position on steps 7 and 12.

Gentleman's Part

Step 1 (Beat 1)

- Facing DW, step forward with the left foot.
- The footwork is heel, toe.
- Start to rise at the end of this step.

Lady's Part

Step 1 (Beat 1)

- Backing DW, step back with the right foot.
- The footwork is toe, heel.
- Start to rise through the body at the end of this step with no foot rise.

(continued)

Open Right Turn   *(continued)*

Gentleman's Part

Step 2 (Beat 2)

- Facing DW, step side and slightly forward with the right foot.
- There is a slight body turn to the right.
- The footwork is toe.
- Continue to rise.

Step 3 (Beat 3)

- Facing DW, step side and slightly forward with the left foot in promenade position (6.7*a*).
- The footwork is toe, heel.
- Up and then lower to a flat foot at the end of the step.

Step 4 (Beat 1)

- Facing DW, step forward with the right foot in promenade position (6.7*b*).
- Start to turn right.
- The footwork is heel, toe.
- Start to rise at the end of this step.

Step 5 (Beat 2)

- Backing DC, step side with the left foot (6.7*c*).
- There is a quarter turn to the right between steps 4 and 5.
- The footwork is toe
- Continue to rise.
- Sway to the right.

Lady's Part

Step 2 (Beat 2)

- Pointing DC, step diagonally back with the left foot.
- There is a quarter turn to the right between steps 1 and 2.
- The footwork is toe.
- Continue to rise.

Step 3 (Beat 3)

- Facing DC, step side and slightly forward with the right foot in promenade position (6.7*a*).
- The footwork is toe, heel.
- Up and then lower to a flat foot at the end of the step.

Step 4 (Beat 1)

- Facing DC and moving LOD, step forward with the left foot (6.7*b*).
- Start to turn right.
- The footwork is heel, toe.
- Start to rise at the end of this step.

Step 5 (Beat 2)

- Pointing LOD, step forward with the right foot (6.7*c*).
- There is an eighth turn to the right between steps 4 and 5.
- The footwork is toe.
- Continue to rise.
- Sway to the left.

Step 6 (Beat 3)

- Backing LOD, step back with the right foot (6.7*d*).
- There is an eighth turn to the right between steps 5 and 6.
- The footwork is toe, heel.
- Up and then lower to a flat foot at the end of this step.
- Sway to the right.

Step 7 (Beat 1)

- Backing LOD, step back with the left foot (6.7*e*).
- Continue to turn to the right.
- The footwork is toe, heel.
- Stay flat on this step.

Step 8 (Beat 2)

- Facing DC, close the right foot to the left foot or heel turn (6.7*f*).
- There is a three-eighths turn to the right between steps 7 and 8.
- The footwork is heel, toe.
- Stay flat and then rise at the end of this step (6.7*g*).

Step 9 (Beat 3)

- Pointing DC, step diagonally forward with the left foot in promenade position (6.7*h*).
- There is a slight body turn to the right.
- The footwork is toe, heel.
- Up and then lower to a flat foot at the end of this step.

Step 6 (Beat 3)

- Facing LOD, step forward with the left foot (6.7*d*).
- The footwork is toe, heel.
- Up and then lower to a flat foot at the end of this step.
- Sway to the left.

Step 7 (Beat 1)

- Facing LOD, step forward with the right foot in outside position (6.7*e*).
- Continue to turn to the right.
- The footwork is heel, toe.
- Start to rise at the end of this step.

Step 8 (Beat 2)

- Backing DC, step side with the left foot (6.7*f*).
- There is a three-eighths turn to the right between steps 7 and 8.
- The footwork is toe.
- Continue to rise (6.7*g*).

Step 9 (Beat 3)

- Pointing center, step to the side with the right foot in promenade position (6.7*h*).
- There is a three-eighths turn to the right between steps 8 and 9.
- The footwork is toe, heel.
- Up and then lower to a flat foot at the end of this step.

(continued)

Open Right Turn *(continued)*

Gentleman's Part

Step 10 (Beat 1)

- Facing DC and moving toward center, step forward and across in promenade position with the right foot (6.7*i*).
- The footwork is heel, toe.
- Start to rise at the end of the step.

Step 11 (Beat 2)

- Facing DC, step side and slightly forward with the left foot (6.7*j*).
- The footwork is toe.
- Continue to rise.
- Sway to the right.

Step 12 (Beat 3)

- Facing DC, step forward with the right foot in outside position and CBMP (6.7*k*).
- The footwork is toe, heel.
- Up and then lower to a flat foot at the end of the step.
- Sway to the right.

Lady's Part

Step 10 (Beat 1)

- Pointing center, step forward and across with the left foot in promenade position (6.7*i*).
- Start to turn left.
- The footwork is heel, toe.
- Start to rise at the end of this step.

Step 11 (Beat 2)

- Backing LOD, step side and slightly back with the right foot (6.7*j*).
- There is a quarter turn to the left between steps 10 and 11.
- The footwork is toe, heel.
- Continue to rise.
- Sway to the left.

Step 12 (Beat 3)

- Backing DC, step back with the left foot in CBMP (6.7*k*).
- There is an eighth turn to the left between steps 11 and 12.
- The footwork is toe, heel.
- Up and then lower to a flat foot at the end of the step.
- Sway to the left.

Figure 6.7 Open right turn: steps *(a)* 3, *(b)* 4, *(c)* 5, *(d)* 6, *(e)* 7, *(f, g)* 8, *(h)* 9, and *(i)* 10. *(continued)*

Open Right Turn   *(continued)*

Figure 6.7   *(continued)* Open right turn: steps *(j)* 11 and *(k)* 12.

Basic Waltz Step Pattern Combinations

Combination #1

Left forward progressive basic—facing DW

Right box turn—turning three-eighths, facing DW

Right forward progressive basic—facing DC

Side by side progressive basic—facing DC and moving LOD

Left box turn—facing center and turning five-eighths to end DW

Single twinkle opening to left—facing DW

Left box turn—facing DC

> See this technique demonstrated on the DVD

Combination #2

Left box turn—turning three-eighths, facing DC

Grapevine—facing DW

Left forward progressive basic—with a little turn, facing DW

Right forward progressive basic—facing LOD

Left forward progressive basic—with a little turn, facing LOD

Right forward progressive basic—facing DC

Left box turn—turning three-eighths, facing DC

Left forward progressive basic—facing DW

Right box turn—turning three-eighths on first half and one-eighth on second half, facing DW and end facing DC of new LOD

Right forward progressive basic—facing DC

Combination #3

Left box turn—turning three-eighths, facing DC
Single twinkle opening to right—facing DW
Grapevine—facing DW
Left forward progressive basic—facing DW
Right box turn—turning three-eighths, facing DW
Right forward progressive basic—facing DC
Left box turn—turning three-eighths, facing DC
Left forward progressive basic—facing DW
Right forward progressive basic—facing DW

Intermediate Waltz Step Pattern Combinations

Combination #1

Open left turn—facing DC
Open right turn—facing DW
Open left turn—facing DC

Note: Move along LOD.

See this technique demonstrated on the DVD

Combination #2

Open left turn—facing DC
Open right turn—facing DW and end facing DW of new LOD
Open right turn—facing DW and turning one-eighth to end facing DC of new LOD
Open left turn—facing DC

Note: In a corner, the open right turn will end DW of new LOD.

CHAPTER 7

American Style Tango

The tango, as danced in America, originated in Europe. It is a combination of music and movements from many countries, including Africa, Argentina, India, and Spain. The Argentineans developed their own style from those combinations and called it Argentine tango, which has been portrayed in many movies and stage shows. Hollywood picked up on the tango movement in the 1920s and made Rudolph Valentino a household name. This chapter teaches American style tango, which is used in social situations and is easier to learn than Argentine tango.

Tango is probably the most recognized of the ballroom dances, mainly because of the music, which at times is driving and energetic and other times soft and sensual. This dance is the most dramatic of all the ballroom dances and can be quite theatrical. The combination of its music and movements portrays excitement, passion, love, and anger, among other emotions. The tango is a combination of slow and quick walking steps, quick turning movements, and slow fan-type movements. The other dances in this book—waltz, foxtrot, and Viennese waltz—have more movement across the floor than tango because of the nature of the step patterns and the principles of swing and rise and fall.

The music is written in 4/4 time, which simply means that the counts are all even. To keep it basic, each step pattern in this chapter is shown in counts of eight and is noted in slows and quicks. A slow is two beats, and a quick is one beat. Even though the step patterns are counted in groups of eight, counting the music is demonstrated on the DVD as it relates to 4/4 time. The actual steps in the book are numbered, and this notation is not related to the beat values. The last three steps of some patterns—quick, quick, slow—are sometimes referred to as a *tango close*. A tango close is used to end most tango step patterns. The closing foot in the tango close for both the man and the lady is drawn in slowly using the inside of the ball of foot so there is no weight change.

The first step in all the promenade step patterns for the man and lady is written as a side step because the direction of movement is side in relation to the standing foot. However, for simplicity on the DVD they are described as forward steps because the first part of the foot to land on the floor is the heel.

There are four main differences between tango and the other dances.

1. Tango does not rise and fall; it is a walking dance with turns.
2. The feet are picked up off the floor slightly and placed; the feet do not roll as in the other dances.
3. There is no sway unless it is called for in a particular step.
4. The body and arms are positioned differently than in the other dances.

The differences in the arm and body positions create a more compact feeling and enable the dancers to turn more quickly, which makes the dance look sharp. When you are first learning the step patterns, it's best to keep your arms in the regular closed dance position. Only use the tango position when you are very comfortable with the dance. Refer to chapters 4 and 5 for descriptions of tango dance position, footwork, and contrary body movement position (CBMP).

Most of the patterns in this chapter are basic social patterns and listed in order of their level of difficulty. Learning them in order will get you moving around the floor as quickly as possible. As you progress through the patterns, you will also find that elements from previous patterns reappear, which is another reason to proceed through the step patterns in the order presented. The final two patterns in the chapter are intermediate variations. To accomplish those, you'll need to have an excellent understanding of dance position and movement from closed position to promenade position. The intermediate patterns may be combined with the beginning patterns in tango. The alignments noted in the practice combinations explain the direction the man faces to begin the step pattern.

Tango Step Patterns

Basic Social

Straight basic

Curved basic

Basic promenade with lady and gentleman turning

Tango rocks

Simple corte

Double corte turning

Left turn

Left turn with fan

Intermediate

Left rock turn with fans

Promenade pivot

STRAIGHT BASIC

See this technique
demonstrated on
the DVD

This pattern will get you started moving down the floor. It travels down the line of dance with no curve or CBMP. During an actual dance its use is limited, but knowledge of it is needed to understand the timing, footwork, and dance position of the tango. The next pattern in the chapter explains how to curve the basic.

Gentleman's Part

Step 1
- Facing line of dance (LOD), step forward with the left foot.
- The footwork is heel.
- The timing is slow (beats 1 and 2).

Step 2
- Facing LOD, step forward with the right foot.
- The footwork is heel.
- The timing is slow (beats 3 and 4).

Step 3
- Facing LOD, step forward with the left foot.
- The footwork is heel.
- The timing is quick (beat 5).

Step 4
- Facing LOD, step side with the right foot.
- The footwork is ball, heel.
- The timing is quick (beat 6).

Step 5
- Facing LOD, close the left foot to the right foot without a weight change (7.1).
- The footwork is inside of ball.
- The timing is slow (beats 7 and 8).

Lady's Part

Step 1
- Backing LOD, step back with the right foot.
- The footwork is ball, heel.
- The timing is slow (beats 1 and 2).

Step 2
- Backing LOD, step back with the left foot.
- The footwork is ball, heel.
- The timing is slow (beats 3 and 4).

Step 3
- Backing LOD, step back on the right foot.
- The footwork is ball, heel.
- The timing is quick (beat 5).

Step 4
- Backing LOD, step side with the left foot.
- The footwork is ball, heel.
- The timing is quick (beat 6).

Step 5
- Backing LOD, close the right foot to the left foot without a weight change (7.1).
- The footwork is inside of ball.
- The timing is slow (beats 7 and 8).

Figure 7.1 Straight basic: step 5.

CURVED BASIC

This pattern will use CBMP to curve the dance around the floor. It can be started at any alignment and will be used much more frequently than the straight basic. Curving walks are characteristic of good tango dancing. When you start curving, check your posture, the body alignments with each other, and arm positions to make the turn easier to control.

See this technique demonstrated on the DVD

Gentleman's Part

Step 1

- Facing diagonal wall (DW), step forward with the left foot in CBMP (7.2*a*).
- The step will start to turn to the left.
- The footwork is heel.
- The timing is slow (beats 1 and 2).

Step 2

- Facing LOD, step forward with the right foot, with the right side leading (7.2*b*).
- There is an eighth turn to the left between steps 1 and 2.
- The footwork is heel.
- The timing is slow (beats 3 and 4).

Lady's Part

Step 1

- Backing DW, step back with the right foot in CBMP (7.2*a*).
- The step will start to turn to the left.
- The footwork is ball, heel.
- The timing is slow (beats 1 and 2).

Step 2

- Backing LOD, step back with the left foot with the left side leading (7.2*b*).
- There is an eighth turn to the left between steps 1 and 2.
- The footwork is ball, heel.
- The timing is slow (beats 3 and 4).

(continued)

Curved Basic   *(continued)*

Gentleman's Part	**Lady's Part**

Gentleman's Part

Step 3

- Facing diagonal center (DC), step forward with the left foot in CBMP.
- There is an eighth turn between steps 2 and 3.
- The footwork is heel.
- The timing is quick (beat 5).

Step 4

- Facing DC, step side with the right foot.
- There is no more turn.
- The footwork is ball, heel.
- The timing is quick (beat 6).

Step 5

- Facing DC, close the left foot to the right foot without a weight change.
- The footwork is inside of ball.
- The timing is slow (beats 7 and 8).

Lady's Part

Step 3

- Backing DC, step back with the right foot in CBMP.
- There is an eighth turn to the left between steps 2 and 3.
- The footwork is ball, heel.
- The timing is quick (beat 5).

Step 4

- Backing DC, step side with the left foot.
- There is no more turn.
- The footwork is ball, heel.
- The timing is quick (beat 6).

Step 5

- Backing DC, close the right foot to the left foot without a weight change.
- The footwork is inside of ball.
- The timing is slow (beats 7 and 8).

Figure 7.2   Curved basic: steps *(a)* 1 and *(b)* 2.

BASIC PROMENADE WITH LADY OR MAN TURNING

A basic promenade can involve either the gentleman or the lady turning from promenade position back to closed position. These figures start in promenade position, so the figure danced before needs to end in promenade. They may be danced at any alignment. These patterns should be studied closely because many tango figures will end with or include part of these patterns.

In tango, it is always easier to open to promenade to the left; however, sometimes promenade will open to the right. The reason it's easier to open to the left is because the feet are close together from the previous tango close step. Be aware of this principle as you dance around the floor.

In the basic promenade with lady turning, the manner in which the lady is closed back to dance position is an important element. At the end of step 2, the man uses his wrist to close the lady as he turns his upper body to the left slightly. The lady makes the complete turn on her left foot before she steps back with the right.

Basic Promenade With Lady Turning

> See this technique demonstrated on the DVD

Gentleman's Part

Step 1

- Facing DW, step side with the left foot in promenade position (7.3*a*).
- The step is moving along LOD.
- The footwork is heel.
- The timing is slow (beats 1 and 2).

Step 2

- Facing LOD, step forward and across with the right foot in CBMP (7.3*b*).
- There is an eighth turn to the left on step 2.
- This step starts in promenade but will end in closed position; the lady is brought back in front of the man (7.3*c*).
- The footwork is heel.
- The timing is slow (beats 3 and 4).

Lady's Part

Step 1

- Facing DC, step side with the right foot in promenade position (7.3*a*).
- The step is moving along LOD.
- The footwork is heel.
- The timing is slow (beats 1 and 2).

Step 2

- Facing DC, step forward with the left foot in promenade position and CBMP (7.3*b*).
- There is three-eighths turn to the left on step 2 to end back in closed position (7.3*c*).
- The footwork is heel.
- The timing is slow (beats 3 and 4).

(continued)

Basic Promenade With Lady Turning   *(continued)*

Gentleman's Part

Step 3
- Facing LOD, step forward with the left foot.
- There is no turn.
- The footwork is heel.
- The timing is quick (beat 5).

Step 4
- Facing LOD, step side with the right foot.
- There is no turn.
- The footwork is ball, heel.
- The timing is quick (beat 6).

Step 5
- Facing LOD, close the left foot to the right foot without a weight change.
- The footwork is inside of ball.
- The timing is slow (beats 7 and 8).

Lady's Part

Step 3
- Backing LOD, step back with the right foot.
- There is no more turn.
- The footwork is ball, heel.
- The timing is quick (beat 5).

Step 4
- Backing LOD, step side with the left foot.
- There is no turn.
- The footwork is ball, heel.
- The timing is quick (beat 6).

Step 5
- Backing LOD, close the right foot to the left foot without a weight change.
- The footwork is inside of ball.
- The timing is slow (beats 7 and 8).

Figure 7.3   Basic promenade with lady turning: steps *(a)* 1 and *(b, c)* 2.

See this technique
demonstrated on
the DVD

Practice Combination

Two straight basics—facing LOD, end in promenade opening to the left in a corner of the room

Basic promenade with lady turning—facing new LOD

Two straight basics—facing LOD

Basic Promenade With Man Turning

Gentleman's Part

Step 1

- Facing DW, step side with the left foot in promenade position.
- The step is moving along LOD.
- The footwork is heel.
- The timing is slow (beats 1 and 2).

Step 2

- Facing DW, step forward with the right foot in promenade position and CBMP (7.4*a*).
- There is three-eighths turn to the right on step 2 to end back in closed position (7.4*b*).
- The footwork is heel.
- The timing is slow (beats 3 and 4).

Step 3

- Backing LOD, step side and slightly back with the left foot.
- This step will start to turn to the right.
- The footwork is ball, heel.
- The timing is quick (beat 5).

Lady's Part

Step 1

- Facing DC, step side with the right foot in promenade position.
- This step moves along LOD.
- The footwork is heel.
- The timing is slow (beats 1 and 2).

Step 2

- Facing LOD, step forward and across with the left foot in promenade position and CBMP (7.4*a*).
- There is an eighth turn to the right on this step (7.4*b*).
- The footwork is heel.
- The timing is slow (beats 3 and 4).

Step 3

- Facing LOD, step forward with the right foot.
- This step will start to turn to the right.
- The footwork is heel.
- The timing is quick (beat 5).

(continued)

Basic Promenade With Man Turning   *(continued)*

Gentleman's Part

Step 4

- Pointing DC, step side with the right foot.
- There is an eighth turn to the right between steps 3 and 4, but the body turns less.
- The footwork is ball, heel.
- The timing is quick (beat 6).

Step 5

- Facing DC, close the left foot to the right foot without a weight change.
- The body completes the turn on this step.
- The footwork is inside of ball.
- The timing is slow (beats 7 and 8).

Lady's Part

Step 4

- Backing DC, step side with the left foot.
- There is an eighth turn to the right between steps 3 and 4.
- The footwork is ball, heel.
- The timing is quick (beat 6).

Step 5

- Backing DC, close the right foot to the left foot without a weight change.
- There is no more turn.
- The footwork is inside of ball.
- The timing is slow (beats 7 and 8).

Figure 7.4   Basic promenade with man turning: step *(a, b)* 2.

See this technique
demonstrated on
the DVD

Practice Combination

Straight basic—facing DW toward a corner of the room, end in promenade opening to the left

Basic promenade with man turning—facing DC of the new line of dance

Straight basic—facing DC

TANGO ROCKS

This pattern can be done in various alignments, but should keep moving in the general line of dance. The rocks are an important element in tango because part of the character of the dance is stopping and starting, which makes it look sharp. Tango rocks may be used any time there is enough space to complete the pattern.

Gentleman's Part

Step 1

- Facing LOD, step forward with the left foot.
- There is no turn over the whole pattern.
- The footwork is heel.
- The timing is slow (beats 1 and 2).

Step 2

- Facing LOD, step forward with the right foot.
- The footwork is heel.
- The timing is slow (beats 3 and 4).

Step 3

- Facing LOD, take a very small step (one foot length) forward with the left foot (7.5a).
- The footwork is heel.
- The timing is quick (beat 5).

Lady's Part

Step 1

- Backing LOD, step back with the right foot.
- The footwork is ball, heel.
- The timing is slow (beats 1 and 2).

Step 2

- Backing LOD, step back with the left foot.
- The footwork is ball, heel.
- The timing is slow (beats 3 and 4).

Step 3

- Backing LOD, take a very small step back (amounting to the same distance that the man moves) with the right foot (7.5a).
- The footwork is ball.
- The timing is quick (beat 5).

(continued)

Tango Rocks   *(continued)*

Gentleman's Part	**Lady's Part**

Step 4

- Facing LOD, replace the weight back to the right foot (7.5*b*).
- The footwork is ball, heel.
- The timing is quick (beat 6).

Step 5

- Facing LOD, step forward with the left foot (7.5*c*).
- The footwork is heel.
- The timing is slow (beats 7 and 8).

Step 6

- Facing LOD, take a very small step (one foot length) forward with the right foot (7.5*d*).
- The footwork is heel.
- The timing is quick (beat 1).

Step 7

- Facing LOD, replace the weight back to the left foot (7.5*e*).
- The footwork is ball, heel.
- The timing is quick (beat 2).

Step 8

- Facing LOD, step forward with the right foot (7.5*f*).
- The footwork is heel.
- The timing is slow (beats 3 and 4).

Step 9

- Facing LOD, step forward with the left foot.
- The footwork is heel.
- The timing is quick (beat 5).

Step 4

- Backing LOD, replace the weight forward to the left foot (7.5*b*).
- The footwork is flat.
- The timing is quick (beat 6).

Step 5

- Backing LOD, step back with the right foot (7.5*c*).
- The footwork is ball, heel.
- The timing is slow (beats 7 and 8).

Step 6

- Backing LOD, take a very small step back (amounting to the same distance that the man moves) with the left foot (7.5*d*).
- The footwork is ball.
- The timing is quick (beat 1).

Step 7

- Backing LOD, replace the weight forward to the right foot (7.5*e*).
- The footwork is flat.
- The timing is quick (beat 2).

Step 8

- Backing LOD, step back on the left foot (7.5*f*).
- The footwork is ball, heel.
- The timing is slow (beats 3 and 4).

Step 9

- Backing LOD, step back with the right foot.
- The footwork is ball, heel.
- The timing is quick (beat 5).

Step 10

- Facing LOD, step side with the right foot.
- The footwork is ball, heel.
- The timing is quick (beat 6).

Step 11

- Facing LOD, close the left foot to the right foot without a weight change.
- The footwork is inside of ball.
- The timing is slow (beats 7 and 8).

Step 10

- Backing LOD, step side with the left foot.
- The footwork is ball, heel.
- The timing is quick (beat 6).

Step 11

- Backing LOD, close the right foot to the left foot without a weight change.
- The footwork is inside of ball.
- The timing is slow (beats 7 and 8).

Figure 7.5 Tango rocks: steps *(a)* 3, *(b)* 4, *(c)* 5, *(d)* 6, *(e)* 7, and *(f)* 8.

Practice Combination

Straight basic—facing LOD

Tango rocks—facing LOD, end in promenade opening to the left in a corner of the room

Basic promenade with lady turning—facing new LOD

Straight basic—facing LOD

Tango rocks—facing LOD

SIMPLE CORTE

See this technique demonstrated on the DVD

The simple corte (pronounced KOR-tay) adds flair to the dance and conveys the image most people have of tango. As the man steps backward on the first step, the lady lunges forward and turns her head to look back over her left shoulder. This position adds a dramatic style to the dance. In this pattern, the man begins by moving backward, so it can be used as an evasive step if another couple moves into your path, or it may be danced as an interesting variation.

Gentleman's Part

Step 1

- Backing against LOD, step back with the left foot, with the left side of the body leading (7.6*a*).
- The footwork is ball, heel.
- The timing is slow (beats 1 and 2).

Step 2

- Facing LOD, step forward with the right foot (7.6*b*).
- The footwork is heel.
- The timing is slow (beats 3 and 4).

Lady's Part

Step 1

- Facing against LOD, step forward with the right foot, with the right side of the body leading (7.6*a*).
- The footwork is heel.
- The timing is slow (beats 1 and 2).

Step 2

- Backing LOD, replace the weight back to the left foot (7.6*b*).
- The footwork is ball, heel.
- The timing is slow (beats 3 and 4).

Step 3

- Facing LOD, step forward with the left foot.
- The footwork is heel.
- The timing is quick (beat 5).

Step 4

- Facing LOD, step side with the right foot.
- The footwork is ball, heel.
- The timing is quick (beat 6).

Step 5

- Facing LOD, close the left foot to the right foot without a weight change.
- The footwork is inside of ball.
- The timing is slow (beats 7 and 8).

Step 3

- Backing LOD, step back on the right foot.
- The footwork is ball, heel.
- The timing is quick (beat 5).

Step 4

- Backing LOD, step side with the left foot.
- The footwork is ball, heel.
- The timing is quick (beat 6).

Step 5

- Backing LOD, close the right foot to the left foot without a weight change.
- The footwork is inside of ball.
- The timing is slow (beats 7 and 8).

Figure 7.6 Simple corte: steps *(a)* 1 and *(b)* 2.

Practice Combination

Straight basic—facing LOD

Simple corte—facing LOD

Tango rocks—facing LOD, end in promenade opening to the left in the corner of a room

Basic promenade with lady turning—facing new LOD

Straight basic—facing LOD

Simple corte—facing LOD

DOUBLE CORTE TURNING

See this technique demonstrated on the DVD

This step pattern is similar to the simple corte, but the turn adds a degree of difficulty. Because there is rotation into the corte, it will look even more dramatic than the simple corte. It is mainly danced to add flair to the dance, but it may be used to avoid another couple. When dancing either corte, be aware of maintaining your dance position in relation to each other and holding the arms still.

Gentleman's Part

Step 1

- Facing DC, step forward with the left foot in CBMP.
- Start turning to the left.
- The footwork is heel.
- The timing is quick (beat 1).

Step 2

- Backing LOD, step back with the right foot in CBMP.
- There is three-eighths turn to the left between steps 1 and 2.
- The footwork is ball, heel.
- The timing is quick (beat 2).

Lady's Part

Step 1

- Backing DC, step back with the right foot in CBMP.
- Start turning to the left.
- The footwork is ball, heel.
- The timing is quick (beat 1).

Step 2

- Facing LOD, step forward with the left foot in CBMP.
- There is three-eighths turn to the left between steps 1 and 2.
- The footwork is heel.
- The timing is quick (beat 2).

Step 3

- Backing LOD, step back with the left foot, with the left side leading.
- There is no turn.
- The footwork is ball, heel.
- The timing is slow (beats 3 and 4).

Step 4

- Facing against LOD, step forward with the right foot.
- There is no turn.
- The footwork is heel.
- The timing is slow (beats 5 and 6).

Step 5

- Facing against LOD, step forward with the left foot in CBMP.
- Start turning to the left.
- The footwork is heel.
- The timing is quick (beat 7).

Step 6

- Backing DC against LOD, step back with the right foot in CBMP.
- There is three-eighths turn to the left between steps 5 and 6.
- The footwork is ball, heel.
- The timing is quick (beat 8).

Step 7

- Backing DC against LOD, step back with the left foot, with the left side leading.
- There is no turn.
- The footwork is ball, heel.
- The timing is slow (beats 1 and 2).

Step 3

- Facing LOD, step forward with the right foot, with the right side leading.
- There is no turn.
- The footwork is heel.
- The timing is slow (beats 3 and 4).

Step 4

- Backing against LOD, replace the weight back to the left foot.
- There is no turn.
- The footwork is ball, heel.
- The timing is slow (beats 5 and 6).

Step 5

- Backing against LOD, step back on the right foot in CBMP.
- Start turning to the left.
- The footwork is ball, heel.
- The timing is quick (beat 7).

Step 6

- Facing DC against LOD, step forward with the left foot in CBMP.
- There is three-eighths turn to the left between steps 5 and 6.
- The footwork is heel.
- The timing is quick (beat 8).

Step 7

- Facing DC against LOD, step forward with the right foot, with the right side leading.
- There is no turn.
- The footwork is heel.
- The timing is slow (beats 1 and 2).

(continued)

Double Corte Turning   *(continued)*

Gentleman's Part

Step 8

- Facing DW, step forward with the right foot.
- There is no more turn in this pattern.
- The footwork is heel.
- The timing is slow (beats 3 and 4).

Step 9

- Facing DW, step forward with the left foot.
- The footwork is heel.
- The timing is quick (beat 5).

Step 10

- Facing DW, step side with the right foot.
- The footwork is ball, heel.
- The timing is quick (beat 6).

Step 11

- Facing DW, close the left foot to the right foot without a weight change.
- The footwork is inside of ball.
- The timing is slow (beats 7 and 8).

Lady's Part

Step 8

- Backing DW, replace the weight back to the left foot.
- There is no more turn in this pattern.
- The footwork is ball, heel.
- The timing is slow (beats 3 and 4).

Step 9

- Backing DW, step back on the right foot.
- The footwork is ball, heel.
- The timing is quick (beat 5).

Step 10

- Backing DW, step side with the left foot.
- The footwork is ball, heel.
- The timing is quick (beat 6).

Step 11

- Backing DW, close the right foot to the left foot without a weight change.
- The footwork is inside of ball.
- The timing is slow (beats 7 and 8).

Practice Combination

Curved basic—facing LOD, end DC

Double corte turning—facing DC, end DW

Curved basic—facing DW, end LOD

Simple corte—facing LOD

LEFT TURN

This pattern uses different timing and movement than the tango patterns presented so far, and it does not end with a normal tango close. This pattern moves down the floor with a stronger turning action than the curved basic, which adds more quickness and sharpness to the dance. Because the ending is different, it has a different look than the basic action. Even though one of the steps in this pattern is in outside position, the outside position applies only to the lower body from the middle of the thigh down to the foot.

See this technique demonstrated on the DVD

Gentleman's Part

Step 1
- Facing DC, step forward with the left foot in CBMP.
- Start turning to the left.
- The footwork is heel.
- The timing is quick (beat 1).

Step 2
- Backing DW, step side with the right foot (7.7*a*).
- There is a quarter turn to the left between steps 1 and 2.
- The footwork is ball, heel.
- The timing is quick (beat 2).

Step 3
- Backing LOD, step back with the left foot in CBMP (7.7*b*).
- There is an eighth turn to the left between steps 2 and 3.
- The footwork is ball, heel.
- The timing is slow (beats 3 and 4).

Step 4
- Backing LOD, step back with the right foot.
- Start turning to the left.
- The footwork is ball, heel.
- The timing is quick (beat 5).

Lady's Part

Step 1
- Backing DC, step back with the right foot in CBMP.
- Start turning to the left.
- The footwork is ball, heel.
- The timing is quick (beat 1).

Step 2
- Pointing LOD, step side and slightly forward with the left foot (7.7*a*).
- There is three-eighths turn to the left between steps 1 and 2.
- The footwork is whole foot.
- The timing is quick (beat 2).

Step 3
- Facing LOD, step forward with the right foot in outside position and CBMP (7.7*b*).
- There is no turn.
- The footwork is heel.
- The timing is slow (beats 3 and 4).

Step 4
- Facing LOD, step forward with the left foot.
- Start turning to the left.
- The footwork is heel.
- The timing is quick (beat 5).

(continued)

Left Turn   *(continued)*

Gentleman's Part

Step 5

- Pointing DW, step side and slightly forward with the left foot (7.7*c*).
- There is three-eighths turn to the left between steps 4 and 5.
- The footwork is inside edge of foot, then whole foot.
- The timing is quick (beat 6).

Step 6

- Facing DW, close the right foot to the left foot.
- There is no turn.
- The footwork is whole foot.
- The timing is slow (beats 7 and 8).

Lady's Part

Step 5

- Backing wall, step side and slightly back with the right foot (7.7*c*).
- There is a quarter turn to the left between steps 4 and 5.
- The footwork is inside edge of foot, then whole foot.
- The timing is quick (beat 6).

Step 6

- Backing DW, close the left foot to the right foot.
- There is an eighth turn to the left between steps 5 and 6.
- The footwork is whole foot.
- The timing is slow (beats 7 and 8).

Figure 7.7   Left turn: steps *(a)* 2, *(b)* 3, and *(c)* 5.

Practice Combination

Curved basic—facing LOD, end DC

Left turn—facing DC, end DW

Curved basic—facing DW, end LOD

Simple corte—facing LOD

Practice Combination

Straight basic—facing DW toward a corner of the room, end in promenade opening to the left

Basic promenade with man turning—facing new LOD, end facing DC

Left turn—facing DC, end DW

Curved basic—facing DW, end DC

Double corte turning—facing DC, end DW

Curved basic—facing DW

LEFT TURN WITH FAN

This pattern starts like the left turn, but ends with the lady doing a fan. A fan is a swiveling action on one foot mainly danced by the lady, although the gentleman does it occasionally. The fan action, which is another characteristic of tango, creates a sensual mood. The purpose

See this technique demonstrated on the DVD

of the pattern is to move down the floor but to end with a different feeling than just dancing the left turn. To practice the fan, walk forward on the right foot, swivel the right foot along with the hips to the right, leaving the inside of the ball of the left foot on the floor and slightly behind the right foot. Walk forward on the left foot, swivel the left foot along with the hips to the left, leaving the inside of the ball of the right foot on the floor and slightly behind the left foot.

To indicate to the lady that she is going to fan, the man turns his upper body to the right as he uses his right hand and wrist to turn her. It is the same exercise as turning the lady to promenade to the right. The lady will respond to the man's turn of his upper body by turning her feet to create the swiveling action. As always, be aware of the relationship of both partner's bodies in dance position.

Gentleman's Part

Step 1
- Facing DC, step forward with the left foot in CBMP.
- Start turning to the left.
- The footwork is heel.
- The timing is quick (beat 1).

Step 2
- Backing DW, step side with the right foot.
- There is a quarter turn to the left between steps 1 and 2.
- The footwork is ball, heel.
- The timing is quick (beat 2).

Step 3
- Backing LOD, step back with the left foot in CBMP.
- There is an eighth turn to the left between steps 2 and 3.
- The footwork is ball, heel.
- The timing is slow (beats 3 and 4).

Step 4
- Backing LOD, step back with the right foot.
- Start turning to the left.
- The footwork is ball, heel.
- The timing is quick (beat 5).

Step 5
- Pointing DW, step side and slightly forward with the left foot.
- There is three-eighths turn to the left between steps 4 and 5.
- The footwork is inside edge of foot, then whole foot.
- The timing is quick (beat 6).

Lady's Part

Step 1
- Backing DC, step back with the right foot in CBMP.
- Start turning to the left.
- The footwork is ball, heel.
- The timing is quick (beat 1).

Step 2
- Pointing LOD, step side and slightly forward with the left foot.
- There is three-eighths turn to the left between steps 1 and 2.
- The footwork is whole foot.
- The timing is quick (beat 2).

Step 3
- Facing LOD, step forward with the right foot in outside position and CBMP.
- There is no turn.
- The footwork is heel.
- The timing is slow (beats 3 and 4).

Step 4
- Facing LOD, step forward with the left foot.
- Start turning to the left.
- The footwork is heel.
- The timing is quick (beat 5).

Step 5
- Backing wall, step side and slightly back with the right foot.
- There is a quarter turn to the left between steps 4 and 5.
- The footwork is ball, heel.
- The timing is quick (beat 6).

Step 6

- Facing DW, step forward with the right foot in outside position and CBMP (7.8*a*).
- There is no turn.
- The footwork is heel.
- The timing is slow (beats 7 and 8).

Step 7

- Backing DC against LOD, replace the weight back to the left foot and end in promenade position (7.8*b, c*).
- There is no more turn in this pattern.
- The footwork is ball, heel.
- The timing is slow (beats 1 and 2).

Step 8

- Facing DW, step forward with the right foot in promenade position and CBMP and end in closed position (7.8*d, e*).
- The footwork is heel.
- The timing is slow (beats 3 and 4).

Step 9

- Facing DW, step forward with the left foot.
- The footwork is heel.
- The timing is quick (beat 5).

Step 6

- Backing DW, step back with the left foot in CBMP (7.8*a*).
- There is an eighth turn to the left between steps 5 and 6.
- The footwork is ball, heel.
- The timing is slow (beats 7 and 8).

Step 7

- Facing DC against LOD, step forward with the right foot in outside position, swivel, and end in promenade position (7.8*b, c*).
- There is three-eighths turn to the right on step 7.
- The footwork is heel and inside of ball of left foot.
- The timing is slow (beats 1 and 2).

Step 8

- Facing LOD, step forward with the left foot in promenade position, swivel, and end in closed position (7.8*d, e*).
- There is three-eighths turn to the left on step 8.
- The footwork is heel and inside of ball of right foot.
- The timing is slow (beats 3 and 4).

Step 9

- Backing DW, step back on the right foot.
- There is no more turn in this pattern.
- The footwork is ball, heel.
- The timing is quick (beat 5).

(continued)

Left Turn With Fan   *(continued)*

Gentleman's Part

Step 10

- Facing DW, step side with the right foot.
- The footwork is ball, heel.
- The timing is quick (beat 6).

Lady's Part

Step 10

- Backing DW, step side with the left foot.
- The footwork is ball, heel.
- The timing is quick (beat 6).

Figure 7.8   Left turn with fan: steps *(a)* 6, *(b, c)* 7, and *(d, e)* 8.

Step 11

- Facing DW, close the left foot to the right foot without a weight change.
- The footwork is inside of ball.
- The timing is slow (beats 7 and 8).

Step 11

- Backing DW, close the right foot to the left foot without a weight change.
- The footwork is inside of ball.
- The timing is slow (beats 7 and 8).

Practice Combination

Curved basic—facing DW, end LOD

Simple corte—facing LOD

Curved basic—facing LOD, end DC

Left turn with fan—facing DC, end DW

Curved basic—facing DW, end LOD

LEFT ROCK TURN WITH FANS

This intermediate pattern begins the same way as the double corte turning, but adds fans. It is more difficult than the left turn with fan or the double corte turning because the turning action has to stop to signal the lady to fan. The lady has to turn left and then quickly change and turn right to create the fan. Even though it is an intermediate-level pattern, it may still be danced along with the beginning dance patterns. This pattern adds more flair and excitement to the dance, but a very good understanding of posture, dance position, and turn is needed to accomplish this pattern with ease.

See this technique demonstrated on the DVD

Gentleman's Part

Step 1

- Facing DC, step forward with the left foot in CBMP.
- Start turning to the left.
- The footwork is heel.
- The timing is quick (beat 1).

Lady's Part

Step 1

- Backing DC, step back with the right foot in CBMP.
- Start turning to the left.
- The footwork is ball, heel.
- The timing is quick (beat 1).

(continued)

Left Rock Turn With Fans *(continued)*

Gentleman's Part

Step 2

- Backing LOD, step back and slightly side with the right foot.
- There is three-eighths turn to the left between steps 1 and 2.
- The footwork is ball, heel.
- The timing is quick (beat 2).

Step 3

- Backing LOD, step back with the left foot in CBMP and end in promenade position.
- There is no turn.
- The footwork is ball, heel.
- The timing is slow (beats 3 and 4).

Step 4

- Facing against LOD, step forward with the right foot in promenade position and end in closed position.
- There is no turn.
- The footwork is heel.
- The timing is slow (beats 5 and 6).

Step 5

- Facing against LOD, step forward with the left foot in CBMP.
- Start turning to the left.
- The footwork is heel.
- The timing is quick (beat 7).

Lady's Part

Step 2

- Pointing LOD, step side and slightly forward with the left foot.
- There is three-eighths turn to the left between steps 1 and 2.
- The footwork is whole foot.
- The timing is quick (beat 2).

Step 3

- Facing LOD, step forward with the right foot in outside position, swivel, and end in promenade position.
- There is three-eighths turn to the right on step 3.
- The footwork is heel and inside of ball of left foot.
- The timing is slow (beats 3 and 4).

Step 4

- Facing DW against LOD, step forward with the left foot in promenade position, swivel, and end in closed position.
- There is three-eighths turn to the left on step 4.
- The footwork is heel and inside of ball of right foot.
- The timing is slow (beats 5 and 6).

Step 5

- Backing against LOD, step back on the right foot in CBMP.
- Start turning to the left.
- The footwork is ball, heel.
- The timing is quick (beat 7).

Step 6

- Backing DC against LOD, step back and slightly side with the right foot.
- There is three-eighths turn to the left between steps 5 and 6.
- The footwork is ball, heel.
- The timing is quick (beat 8).

Step 7

- Backing DC against LOD, step back with the left foot in CBMP and end in promenade position.
- There is no turn.
- The footwork is ball, heel.
- The timing is slow (beats 1 and 2).

Step 8

- Facing DW, step forward with the right foot in promenade position and end in closed position.
- There is no turn.
- The footwork is heel.
- The timing is slow (beats 3 and 4).

Step 9

- Facing DW, step forward with the left foot.
- The footwork is heel.
- The timing is quick (beat 5).

Step 6

- Pointing DC against LOD, step side and slightly forward with the left foot.
- There is three-eighths turn to the left between steps 5 and 6.
- The footwork is whole foot.
- The timing is quick (beat 8).

Step 7

- Facing DC against LOD, step forward with the right foot in outside position, swivel, and end in promenade position.
- There is three-eighths turn to the right on step 7.
- The footwork is heel and inside of ball of left foot.
- The timing is slow (beats 1 and 2).

Step 8

- Facing LOD, step forward with the left foot in promenade position, swivel, and end in closed position.
- There is three-eighths turn to the left on step 8.
- The footwork is heel and inside of ball of right foot.
- The timing is slow (beats 3 and 4).

Step 9

- Backing DW, step back on the right foot.
- There is no more turn in this pattern.
- The footwork is ball, heel.
- The timing is quick (beat 5).

(continued)

Left Rock Turn With Fans　*(continued)*

Gentleman's Part	Lady's Part
Step 10	**Step 10**
• Facing DW, step side with the right foot.	• Backing DW, step side with the left foot.
• The footwork is ball, heel.	• The footwork is ball, heel.
• The timing is quick (beat 6).	• The timing is quick (beat 6).
Step 11	**Step 11**
• Facing DW, close the left foot to the right foot without a weight change.	• Backing DW, close the right foot to the left foot without a weight change.
• The footwork is inside of ball.	• The footwork is inside of ball.
• The timing is slow (beats 7 and 8).	• The timing is slow (beats 7 and 8).

PROMENADE PIVOT

See this technique demonstrated on the DVD

The promenade pivot turns and moves down the line of dance very quickly. Everyone loves to watch couples dance pivots because when danced well, the couple shows a free and easy movement, and the pattern is showy. The pattern can be used to move down the line of dance, or it may be danced around a corner. It starts in promenade position, so the basic rules for getting to promenade apply. A very good understanding of dance position and posture is needed to make this pattern look effortless.

Gentleman's Part	Lady's Part
Step 1	**Step 1**
• Facing DW and moving LOD, step side with the left foot in promenade position.	• Facing DC and moving LOD, step side with the right foot in promenade position.
• There is no turn.	• There is no turn.
• The footwork is heel.	• The footwork is heel.
• The timing is slow (beats 1 and 2).	• The timing is slow (beats 1 and 2).

Step 2

- Facing DW, step forward with the right foot in promenade position and end backing LOD.
- There is three-eighths turn to the right on step 2.
- The footwork is heel, ball.
- The timing is slow (beats 3 and 4).

Step 3

- Backing LOD step side and slightly back with the left foot (7.9*a*), pivoting and end facing LOD.
- There is a half turn to the right on step 3.
- The footwork is ball, heel.
- The timing is quick (beat 5).

Step 4

- Facing LOD, step forward with the right foot in CBMP (7.9*b*) and end backing DC.
- There is three-eighths turn to the right on step 4.
- The footwork is heel, ball.
- The timing is quick (beat 6).

Step 5

- Backing DC, step side and slightly back with the left foot.
- There is no turn.
- The footwork is ball, heel.
- The timing is slow (beats 7 and 8).

Step 2

- Facing LOD, step forward and across with the left foot in promenade position.
- There is an eighth turn to the right between steps 1 and 2.
- The footwork is heel.
- The timing is slow (beats 3 and 4).

Step 3

- Facing LOD, step forward with the right foot (7.9*a*) and end backing LOD.
- There is a half turn to the right on step 3.
- The footwork is heel, ball.
- The timing is quick (beat 5).

Step 4

- Backing LOD step side and slightly back with the left foot (7.9*b*), pivoting to end facing DC.
- There is three-eighths turn to the right on step 4.
- The footwork is ball, heel.
- The timing is quick (beat 6).

Step 5

- Facing DC, step diagonally forward with the right foot.
- There is no turn.
- The footwork is heel.
- The timing is slow (beats 7 and 8).

(continued)

Promenade Pivot   *(continued)*

Gentleman's Part	Lady's Part

Step 6

- Backing DC, step back with the right foot in CBMP (7.9*c*).
- Start turning to the left.
- The footwork is ball, heel.
- The timing is quick (beat 1).

Step 7

- Pointing DW, step side and slightly forward with the left foot (7.9*d*).
- There is a quarter turn to the left between steps 6 and 7.
- The footwork is inside edge of foot, then whole foot.
- The timing is quick (beat 2).

Step 8

- Facing DW, close the right foot to the left foot (7.9*e*).
- There is no more turn in this pattern.
- The footwork is whole foot.
- The timing is slow (beats 3 and 4).

Step 9

- Facing DW, step forward with the left foot.
- The footwork is heel.
- The timing is quick (beat 5).

Step 10

- Facing DW, step side with the right foot.
- The footwork is ball, heel.
- The timing is quick (beat 6).

Step 6

- Facing DC, step forward with the left foot in CBMP (7.9*c*).
- Start to turn to the left.
- The footwork is heel.
- The timing is quick (beat 1).

Step 7

- Backing DW, step side and slightly back with the right foot (7.9*d*).
- There is a quarter turn to the left between steps 6 and 7.
- The footwork is inside edge of foot, then whole foot.
- The timing is quick (beat 2).

Step 8

- Backing DW, close the left foot to the right foot (7.9*e*).
- There is no more turn in this pattern.
- The footwork is whole foot.
- The timing is slow (beats 3 and 4).

Step 9

- Backing DW, step back on the right foot.
- The footwork is ball, heel.
- The timing is quick (beat 5).

Step 10

- Backing DW, step side with the left foot.
- The footwork is ball, heel.
- The timing is quick (beat 6).

Step 11

- Facing DW, close the left foot to the right foot without a weight change.
- The footwork is inside of ball.
- The timing is slow (beats 7 and 8).

Step 11

- Backing DW, close the right foot to the left foot without a weight change.
- The footwork is inside of ball.
- The timing is slow (beats 7 and 8).

Figure 7.9 Promenade pivot: steps *(a)* 3, *(b)* 4, *(c)* 6, *(d)* 7, and *(e)* 8.

Basic Tango Step Pattern Combinations

Combination #1

See this technique demonstrated on the DVD

Straight basic—facing LOD

Simple corte—facing LOD

Tango rocks—facing LOD and end in promenade opening to the left in the corner of a room

Basic promenade with lady turning—facing new LOD

Straight basic—facing LOD

Simple corte—facing LOD

Curved basic—facing LOD and end DC

Combination #2

Curved basic—facing DW and end LOD

Simple corte—facing LOD

Curved basic—facing LOD and end DC

Left turn—facing DC and end DW

Curved basic—facing DW and end DC

Double corte turning—facing DC

Combination #3

Curved basic—facing DW and end DC

Double corte turning—facing DC and end DW

Curved basic—facing DW and end DC

Left turn with fan—facing DC and end DW

Straight basic—facing DW and end in promenade opening to the left in the corner of the room

Basic promenade with man turning—facing DW of new LOD and end facing DC

Simple corte—facing DC

Tango rocks—facing DC

Intermediate Tango Step Pattern Combinations

Combination #1

See this technique demonstrated on the DVD

Straight basic—facing DW toward a corner of the room and end in promenade opening to the left

Basic promenade with man turning—facing DW and end DC of new LOD

Left turn with fan—facing DC and end DW

Curved basic—facing DW and end DC

Double corte turning—facing DC and end DW

Curved basic—facing DW and end DC of new LOD

Left rock turn with fans—facing DC and end DW

Curved basic—facing DW and end LOD

Combination #2

Curved basic—facing LOD and end DC

Simple corte—facing DC

Left turn—facing DC and end DW

Straight basic—facing DW and end in promenade opening to the left in the corner of the room

Promenade pivot—facing DW of new LOD and end DW

Curved basic—facing DW and end LOD of new line in promenade position opening left

Basic promenade with lady turning—facing DC and end DC

Left rock turn with fans—facing DC and end DW

American Style Foxtrot

The foxtrot is the foundation for most social dances and is probably the easiest dance to learn. It principally walks forward, backward, and to the side. Foxtrot can be danced to many popular songs as well as to classic standards, so it's easily recognizable. The music can have anything from a romantic to a jazzy feel. It's heard in the classics sung by Frank Sinatra and slow dances played in nightclubs today. It is the main type of slow music played at dinner dances, weddings, and nightclubs.

The music is written in 4/4 time, which means there are four beats to a bar of music. Just like in tango, a slow is two beats and a quick is one beat. The basic pattern is done to six counts of music, and some of the step patterns are counted in groups of eight. However, counting the music is demonstrated on the DVD as it relates to 4/4 time. The actual steps taken are numbered, as in the other dances, and these numbers are not related to the beat values.

Foxtrot is the only smooth ballroom dance that originated in the United States, and it is danced all over the world. Many dance historians believe that the dance was named after Harry Fox, an American comedian who used a special trotting step in his vaudeville act. Over the years, the trotting has been eliminated and the dance has become smooth, gliding, and graceful.

Like the waltz, the foxtrot has rise and fall. Foxtrot rise and fall happens at different times than it does in the waltz, and it is not as evident. In the basic steps, it is very slight, and it is more pronounced in the intermediate patterns. When the lady is moving backward, she will never use foot rise; the footwork for every backward step for the lady is toe, heel, even if there is a body rise. As you begin learning, study where the feet are positioned and the amount of turn. When you understand that, you can add the rise and fall. Foxtrot uses several types of rise and fall:

- Figures that move forward with a slow, slow, quick, quick rhythm—Rise slightly at the end of step 2, up on step 3, lower at the end of step 3, and down on step 4.
- Figures that move backward with a slow, slow, quick, quick rhythm—Rise slightly through the body at the end of 2 with no foot rise, up on 3, lower at the end of 3, and down on 4.

- Figures that move forward with a slow, quick, quick rhythm—Rise at the end of 1, up on 2, up on 3, and lower at the end of 3.
- Figures that move backward with a slow, quick, quick rhythm—Rise through the body at the end of 1 with no foot rise, up on 2, up on 3, and lower at the end of 3.
- Figures that move only to the side with a quick, quick rhythm—Rise slightly on 1, lower at the end of 1, and down on 2.

A brushing action in many of the foxtrot step patterns is unique to this dance style. This helps keep you in time with the music and with your partner and helps complete weight changes. During this brushing action, you move the free foot alongside the standing foot with no weight change. A brush is used when changing direction from forward to side, backward to side, forward to backward, and backward to forward. To practice this brushing action, walk forward on your left foot, bring your right foot under your body and close to your left foot, then step to the right. Repeat with walking forward on the right foot. Then walk backward on your left foot, bring your right foot under your body and close to your left foot, then step to the right. Repeat with walking backward on the right foot.

Note: The first step in all the promenade step patterns for the man and lady is written as a side step because the direction of movement is side in relation to the standing foot. However, for simplicity on the DVD they are described as forward steps because the first part of the foot to land on the floor is the heel.

As in the other dances in this book, the step patterns are listed from easiest to most difficult in order to get you moving around the floor as soon as possible. As you progress through the patterns, you will find that elements from previous patterns reappear, so it's best to proceed through the step patterns in the order presented. The intermediate patterns of open left turn and running steps are included at the end of the chapter, but like in waltz, the intermediate patterns should not be combined with the basic patterns. Refer to chapters 4 and 5 for correct posture and dance position, including promenade position and outside position, CBM, and CBMP. Sway is explained in chapter 5 and is used in a few foxtrot step patterns. The terms heel, ball, and toe are used to describe footwork. The details of footwork and foot position are explained in chapter 4. The alignments noted in the practice combinations are all written to explain the direction the man faces to begin the step pattern.

Foxtrot Step Patterns

Basic Social

Forward basic

Left turn—with no turn, turning one-quarter

Turning basic

Chasse

Promenade

Promenade with underarm turn

Grapevine

Promenade pivot

Intermediate Step Patterns

Open left turn

Running steps

FORWARD BASIC

See this technique demonstrated on the DVD

This pattern will get you started moving around the floor. It travels down the line of dance but is mainly used as a teaching aid. In an actual dance situation, the forward basic might be danced occasionally, but rarely in groups or in succession. So during an actual dance its use is limited, but knowledge of it is needed to understand the timing, footwork, and dance position of all the foxtrot patterns. In this pattern, there is a brushing action between steps 2 and 3.

Gentleman's Part

Step 1

- Facing line of dance (LOD), step forward with the left foot.
- The footwork is heel.
- There is no rise on this step.
- The timing is slow (beats 1 and 2).

Lady's Part

Step 1

- Backing LOD, step back with the right foot.
- The footwork is toe, heel.
- There is no rise.
- The timing is slow (beats 1 and 2).

Step 2

- Facing LOD, step forward with the right foot.
- The footwork is heel, toe.
- There is a slight rise at the end of this step.
- The timing is slow (beats 3 and 4).

Step 3

- Facing LOD, step side with the left foot.
- The footwork is toe, heel.
- The rise is up, then lower at the end of the step.
- The timing is quick (beat 5).

Step 4

- Facing LOD, close the right foot to the left foot.
- The footwork is toe, heel.
- Stay down on this step.
- The timing is quick (beat 6).

Step 2

- Backing LOD, step back with the left foot.
- The footwork is toe, heel.
- There is a slight body rise at the end of this step but no foot rise.
- The timing is slow (beats 3 and 4).

Step 3

- Backing LOD, step side with the right foot.
- The footwork is toe, heel.
- The rise is up, then lower at the end of the step.
- The timing is quick (beat 5).

Step 4

- Backing LOD, close the left foot to the right foot.
- The footwork is toe, heel.
- Stay down on this step.
- The timing is quick (beat 6).

LEFT TURN

The left turn is one of the most important steps in foxtrot. Not really considered a traveling step, it is used to change the direction of the dance in a corner or as an evasive step. It is mostly used to turn a quarter of a turn, but it can also be turned less if needed and started at different alignments. It can even be done without turning to keep the timing and movement going if another couple moves in the way. It will be explained first without turn, and then with a quarter turn. In both patterns, there is a brushing action between steps 1 and 2 and between steps 2 and 3. When the lady is moving backward, she will never use foot rise; the footwork for every backward step for the lady is toe, heel, even if there is body rise.

The practice combination at the end of the left turn pattern shows how to put the left turn and forward basic together. It's best to practice these two patterns together before moving on. The combination will help you understand the rhythm of the dance, how the dance moves around the floor, and how to turn in the corners.

See this technique demonstrated on the DVD

Left Turn With No Turn

Gentleman's Part

Step 1
- Facing LOD, step forward with the left foot (8.1*a*).
- The footwork is heel.
- There is no rise.
- The timing is slow (beats 1 and 2).

Step 2
- Backing against LOD, step back with the right foot (8.1*b*).
- The footwork is toe, heel.
- There is a slight body rise at the end of this step but no foot rise.
- The timing is slow (beats 3 and 4).

Step 3
- Facing LOD, step side with the left foot.
- The footwork is toe, heel.
- The rise is up, then lower at the end of the step.
- The timing is quick (beat 5).

Step 4
- Facing LOD, close the right foot to the left foot.
- The footwork is toe, heel.
- Stay down on this step.
- The timing is quick (beat 6).

Lady's Part

Step 1
- Backing LOD, step back with the right foot (8.1*a*).
- The footwork is toe, heel.
- There is no rise.
- The timing is slow (beats 1 and 2).

Step 2
- Facing against LOD, step forward with the left foot (8.1*b*).
- The footwork is heel, toe.
- There is a slight rise at the end of this step.
- The timing is slow (beats 3 and 4).

Step 3
- Backing LOD, step side with the right foot.
- The footwork is toe, heel.
- The rise is up, then lower at the end of the step.
- The timing is quick (beat 5).

Step 4
- Backing LOD, close the left foot to the right foot.
- The footwork is toe, heel.
- Stay down on this step.
- The timing is quick (beat 6).

Figure 8.1 Left turn with no turn: steps *(a)* 1 and *(b)* 2.

See this technique demonstrated on the DVD

Left Turn With a Quarter Turn

Gentleman's Part

Step 1

- Facing LOD, step forward with the left foot.
- There is no turn.
- The footwork is heel.
- There is no rise.
- The timing is slow (beats 1 and 2).

Step 2

- Backing against LOD, step back with the right foot.
- Start to turn left.
- The footwork is toe, heel.
- There is a slight body rise at the end of this step but no foot rise.
- The timing is slow (beats 3 and 4).

Step 3

- Pointing center, step side with the left foot.

Lady's Part

Step 1

- Backing LOD, step back with the right foot.
- There is no turn.
- The footwork is toe, heel.
- There is no rise.
- The timing is slow (beats 1 and 2).

Step 2

- Facing against LOD, step forward with the left foot.
- Start to turn left.
- The footwork is heel, toe.
- There is a slight rise at the end of this step.
- The timing is slow (beats 3 and 4).

Step 3

- Backing center, step side with the right foot.

(continued)

Left Turn With a Quarter Turn   *(continued)*

Gentleman's Part

- There is a quarter turn to the left between steps 2 and 3.
- The footwork is toe, heel.
- The rise is up, then lower at the end of the step.
- The timing is quick (beat 5).

Step 4

- Facing center, close the right foot to the left foot.
- There is no turn.
- The footwork is toe, heel.
- Stay down on this step.
- The timing is quick (beat 6).

Lady's Part

- There is a quarter turn to the left between steps 2 and 3.
- The footwork is toe, heel.
- The rise is up, then lower at the end of the step.
- The timing is quick (beat 5).

Step 4

- Backing center, close the left foot to the right foot.
- The footwork is toe, heel.
- Stay down on this step.
- The timing is quick (beat 6).

Practice Combination

Two forward basics

Left turn—turning a quarter to face the new LOD (If you can't make a quarter turn in one pattern, then dance two left turn patterns turning an eighth on each one.)

Two forward basics

Left turn—turning a quarter to face the new LOD

(Repeat two more times to make one complete turn and end facing where you started.)

TURNING BASIC

See this technique demonstrated on the DVD

This popular step pattern is the basic step of the foxtrot. It moves the dancer around the floor because it travels down the line of dance in a zigzag pattern. The pattern can be danced all around the dance floor.

In a corner, the forward part of the pattern may be turned an eighth of a turn instead of the quarter that is noted, or the backward part turned three-eighths of a turn instead of a quarter turn to move to the correct alignment, which is diagonal wall, to begin the pattern again. The turning basic has a nice feeling of turning and moving forward and backward. In this pattern, there is a brushing action between steps 2 and 3 and between steps 6 and 7.

Gentleman's Part

Step 1

- Facing diagonal wall (DW), step forward with the left foot.
- There is no turn.
- The footwork is heel.
- There is no rise.
- The timing is slow (beats 1 and 2).

Step 2

- Facing DW, step forward with the right foot.
- Start to turn to the right.
- The footwork is heel, toe.
- There is a slight rise at the end of this step.
- The timing is slow (beats 3 and 4).

Step 3

- Backing diagonal center (DC), step side with the left foot.
- There is a quarter turn to the right between steps 2 and 3.
- The footwork is toe, heel.
- The rise is up, then lower at the end of this step.
- The timing is quick (beat 5).

Step 4

- Backing DC, close the right foot to the left foot.
- There is no turn.
- The footwork is toe, heel.
- Stay down on this step.
- The timing is quick (beat 6).

Lady's Part

Step 1

- Backing DW, step back with the right foot.
- There is no turn.
- The footwork is toe, heel.
- There is no rise.
- The timing is slow (beats 1 and 2).

Step 2

- Backing DW, step back with the left foot.
- Start to turn to the right.
- The footwork is toe, heel.
- There is a slight body rise at the end of this step but no foot rise.
- The timing is slow (beats 3 and 4).

Step 3

- Pointing DC, step side with the right foot.
- There is a quarter turn to the right between steps 2 and 3.
- The footwork is toe, heel.
- The rise is up, then lower at the end of this step.
- The timing is quick (beat 5).

Step 4

- Facing DC, close the left foot to the right foot.
- There is no turn.
- The footwork is toe, heel.
- Stay down on this step.
- The timing is quick (beat 6).

(continued)

Turning Basic *(continued)*

Gentleman's Part

Step 5

- Backing DC, step back with the left foot.
- There is no turn.
- The footwork is toe, heel.
- There is no rise.
- The timing is slow (beats 7 and 8).

Step 6

- Backing DC, step back with the right foot.
- Start to turn to the left.
- The footwork is toe, heel.
- There is a slight body rise at the end of this step but no foot rise.
- The timing is slow (beats 1 and 2).

Step 7

- Pointing DW, step side with the left foot.
- There is a quarter turn to the left between steps 6 and 7.
- The footwork is toe, heel.
- The rise is up, then lower at the end of this step.
- The timing is quick (beat 3).

Step 8

- Facing DW, close the right foot to the left foot.
- There is no turn.
- The footwork is toe, heel.
- Stay down on this step.
- The timing is quick (beat 4).

Lady's Part

Step 5

- Facing DC, step forward with the right foot.
- There is no turn.
- The footwork is heel.
- There is no rise.
- The timing is slow (beats 7 and 8).

Step 6

- Facing DC, step forward with the left foot.
- Start to turn to the left.
- The footwork is heel, toe.
- There is a slight rise at the end of this step.
- The timing is slow (beats 1 and 2).

Step 7

- Backing DW, step side with the right foot.
- There is a quarter turn to the left between steps 6 and 7.
- The footwork is toe, heel.
- The rise is up, then lower at the end of this step.
- The timing is quick (beat 3).

Step 8

- Backing DW, close the left foot to the right foot.
- There is no turn.
- The footwork is toe, heel.
- Stay down on this step.
- The timing is quick (beat 4).

CHASSE

The chasse (pronounced sha-SAY) is an easy step variation in the foxtrot that can be used anywhere on the dance floor and at almost any time. It is the side step of the basic pattern and can be repeated as many times as necessary. Because of its simplicity, it can be used to get away from a traffic jam on the floor or to express a rhythm different from the basic slow, slow, quick, quick. It can be done in any alignment and can curve slightly in either direction. It is explained in a straight line, but the dancer can add a sixteenth to an eighth of a curve on the side step before the feet come together.

See this technique demonstrated on the DVD

Gentleman's Part

Step 1

- Facing LOD, step side with the left foot.
- There is no turn.
- The footwork is toe, heel.
- The rise is slight, then lower at the end of this step.
- The timing is quick (beat 1).

Step 2

- Facing LOD, close the right foot to the left foot.
- There is no turn.
- The footwork is toe, heel.
- Stay down on this step.
- The timing is quick (beat 2).

Lady's Part

Step 1

- Backing LOD, step side with the right foot.
- There is no turn.
- The footwork is toe, heel.
- The rise is slight, then lower at the end of this step.
- The timing is quick (beat 1).

Step 2

- Backing LOD, close the left foot to the right foot.
- There is no turn.
- The footwork is toe, heel.
- Stay down on this step.
- The timing is quick (beat 2).

PROMENADE

See this technique demonstrated on the DVD

The promenade is probably one of the most recognizable foxtrot patterns. It moves the dancer down the line of dance and adds interest. The pattern is unique because both partners move in a forward direction, and it has a casual look as if the couple were just strolling along. At the end of the preceding step, the couple will turn to promenade position, as explained in chapter 5. There is a brushing action between steps 2 and 3.

Gentleman's Part

Step 1

- Facing DW and moving LOD, step side with the left foot in promenade position (8.2*a*).
- There is no turn.
- The footwork is heel.
- There is no rise.
- The timing is slow (beats 1 and 2).

Step 2

- Facing DW and moving LOD, step forward and across in CBMP and promenade position with the right foot (8.2*b*).
- Start to turn to the right.
- The footwork is heel, toe.
- There is a slight rise at the end of this step.
- The timing is slow (beats 3 and 4).

Step 3

- Facing wall, step side with the left foot (8.2*c*).
- There is an eighth turn to the right between steps 2 and 3.
- The footwork is toe, heel.
- The rise is up, then lower at the end of this step.
- The timing is quick (beat 5).

Lady's Part

Step 1

- Facing DC and moving LOD, step side with the right foot in promenade position (8.2*a*).
- There is no turn.
- The footwork is heel.
- There is no rise.
- The timing is slow (beats 1 and 2).

Step 2

- Facing DC and moving LOD, step forward and across in CBMP and promenade position with the left foot (8.2*b*).
- Start to turn to the left.
- The footwork is heel, toe.
- There is a slight rise at the end of this step.
- The timing is slow (beats 3 and 4).

Step 3

- Backing wall, step side with the right foot (8.2*c*).
- There is an eighth turn to the left between steps 2 and 3.
- The footwork is toe, heel.
- The rise is up, then lower at the end of this step.
- The timing is quick (beat 5).

Step 4

- Facing wall, close the right foot to the left foot.
- There is no turn.
- The footwork is toe, heel.
- Stay down on this step.
- The timing is quick (beat 6).

Step 4

- Backing wall, close the left foot to the right foot.
- There is no turn.
- The footwork is toe, heel.
- Stay down on this step.
- The timing is quick (beat 6).

Figure 8.2 Promenade: steps *(a)* 1, *(b)* 2, and *(c)* 3.

PROMENADE WITH UNDERARM TURN

This variation of the promenade is fun for the woman. The man dances the basic promenade, but the lady dances an underarm turn. It can be used to travel down the line of dance or just as a flashy variation. The man will raise his left arm at the end of step 2 to indicate to the lady to dance an underarm turn to the right. The lady needs to release her left hand from dance position as the man raises his left arm to turn her. Her hand should move in front of her body as she starts the turn. To accomplish the turn with ease, the lady should pull her center in as she starts to turn. (For more about using the center, see chapter 4.) The man and woman will come back to closed position at the end of step 4. Another promenade should always be danced at the end of the promenade with underarm turn. This is demonstrated on the DVD. In this pattern, there is a brushing action between steps 2 and 3.

See this technique demonstrated on the DVD

Gentleman's Part

Step 1

- Facing DW and moving LOD, step side with the left foot in promenade position.
- There is no turn.
- The footwork is heel.
- There is no rise.
- The timing is slow (beats 1 and 2).

Step 2

- Facing DW and moving LOD, step forward and across in CBMP and promenade position with the right foot.
- Start to turn to the right.
- The footwork is heel, toe.
- There is a slight rise at the end of this step.
- The timing is slow (beats 3 and 4).

Step 3

- Facing wall, step side with the left foot (8.3*a*).
- There is an eighth turn to the right between steps 2 and 3 (8.3*b*).
- The footwork is toe, heel.
- The rise is up, then lower at the end of this step.
- The timing is quick (beat 5).

Step 4

- Facing wall, close the right foot to the left foot (8.3*c*).
- There is no turn.
- The footwork is toe, heel.
- Stay down on this step.
- The timing is quick (beat 6).

Lady's Part

Step 1

- Facing DC and moving LOD, step side with the right foot in promenade position.
- There is no turn.
- The footwork is heel.
- There is no rise.
- The timing is slow (beats 1 and 2).

Step 2

- Facing DC and moving LOD, step forward and across in CBMP and promenade position with the left foot.
- There is no turn.
- The footwork is heel.
- There is no rise.
- The timing is slow (beats 3 and 4).

Step 3

- Facing LOD, step forward with the right foot (8.3*a*).
- There is a half turn to the right on this step (8.3*b*).
- The footwork is heel, toe.
- There is a slight rise on this step.
- The timing is quick (beat 5).

Step 4

- Backing LOD, close the left foot to the right foot (8.3*c*).
- There is a half turn to the right on this step.
- The footwork is toe, heel.
- Lower on this step.
- The timing is quick (beat 6).

Figure 8.3 Promenade with underarm turn: steps *(a, b)* 3 and *(c)* 4.

Practice Combination

Turning basic—facing DW

Three chasses—facing DW

Two turning basics—facing DW

Left turn—facing DW and turning one-eighth to end facing LOD

Promenade with underarm turn—moving along the new LOD

Promenade

Left turn—facing wall and turning one-eighth to end DW

Two chasses—facing DW

Turning basic—facing DW

GRAPEVINE

The grapevine is a nice moving pattern because the feet do not come together at the end, and the timing changes. More room is needed to accomplish this step because it moves more and faster than any of the other patterns learned so far. It is a showy step variation in the foxtrot.

See this technique demonstrated on the DVD

Because it introduces outside position on the left and the right sides, this pattern is more difficult. To accomplish the grapevine with ease, posture and dance position are important. Slight turn in the upper body enables the couple to stay in dance position even though their feet are stepping in outside position. The head positions for both the gentleman and lady should remain in closed dance position. The heads should not turn with the body.

There will be more quicks than slows, so the pattern will move faster down the floor, giving it a more exciting look and feel. The four quicks may also be repeated for a longer grapevine action. Start again with step 3 and repeat until step 6 for a total of eight quicks.

Gentleman's Part

Step 1

- Facing DW, step forward with the left foot in outside position (8.4*a*).
- There is no turn.
- The footwork is heel
- There is no rise.
- The timing is slow (beats 1 and 2).

Step 2

- Facing DW, step forward with the right foot in outside position (8.4*b*).
- Start to turn to the right.
- The footwork is heel, toe.
- There is a slight rise at the end of this step.
- The timing is slow (beats 3 and 4).

Step 3

- Backing DC, step side with the left foot (8.4*c*).
- There is a quarter turn to the right between steps 2 and 3.
- The footwork is toe, heel.
- The rise is up on this step.
- The timing is quick (beat 5).

Lady's Part

Step 1

- Backing DW, step back with the right foot (8.4*a*).
- There is no turn.
- The footwork is toe, heel.
- There is no rise.
- The timing is slow (beats 1 and 2).

Step 2

- Backing DW, step back with the left foot (8.4*b*).
- Start to turn to the right.
- The footwork is toe, heel.
- There is a slight body rise at the end of this step with no foot rise.
- The timing is slow (beats 3 and 4).

Step 3

- Facing DC, step side and slightly forward with the right foot (8.4*c*).
- There is a quarter turn to the right between steps 2 and 3.
- The footwork is toe, heel.
- The rise is up, then lower at the end of the step.
- The timing is quick (beat 5).

Step 4

- Backing DC, step back with the right foot in CBMP (8.4*d*).
- Start to turn to the left.
- The footwork is toe.
- The rise is at the end of this step.
- The timing is quick (beat 6).

Step 5

- Pointing DW, step side and slightly forward with the left foot (8.4*e*).
- There is a quarter turn to the left between steps 4 and 5.
- The footwork is toe, heel.
- The rise is up, then lower at the end of this step.
- The timing is quick (beat 7).

Step 6

- Facing DW, step forward with the right foot in outside position (8.4*f*).
- There is no turn.
- The footwork is heel.
- There is no rise.
- The timing is quick (beat 8).

Step 4

- Facing DC, step forward in outside position with the left foot on the partner's left side (8.4*d*).
- Start to turn to the left.
- The footwork is heel, toe.
- There is a slight rise at the end of this step.
- The timing is quick (beat 6).

Step 5

- Backing DW, step side and slightly back with the right foot (8.4*e*).
- There is a quarter turn to the left between steps 4 and 5.
- The footwork is toe, heel.
- The rise is up, then lower at the end of this step.
- The timing is quick (beat 7).

Step 6

- Backing DW, step back with the left foot in CBMP (8.4*f*).
- There is no turn.
- The footwork is toe, heel.
- There is no rise.
- The timing is quick (beat 8).

(continued)

Grapevine *(continued)*

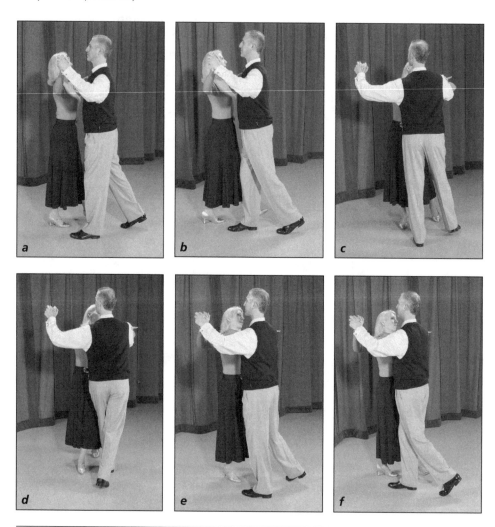

Figure 8.4 Grapevine: steps *(a)* 1, *(b)* 2, *(c)* 3, *(d)* 4, *(e)* 5, and *(f)* 6.

PROMENADE PIVOT

See this technique demonstrated on the DVD

This pattern starts in promenade position and has a pivoting action in the middle of it. It moves the dancers down the floor and also looks flashy because of the quick turn of the pivot. Keep the right foot in front of the left foot as you dance the pivot. Both partners need to keep their heads in closed dance position during the pivot. There is a brushing action between steps 6 and 7.

Gentleman's Part

Step 1

- Facing DW and moving LOD, step side with the left foot in promenade position.
- There is no turn.
- The footwork is heel.
- There is no rise.
- The timing is slow (beats 1 and 2).

Step 2

- Facing DW and moving LOD, step forward in CBMP and promenade position with the right foot.
- There is three-eighths turn to the right.
- The footwork is heel, toe.
- There is no rise.
- The timing is slow (beats 3 and 4).

Step 3

- Backing LOD step to the side and slightly back with the left foot (8.5*a*), pivoting and end facing LOD.
- There is a half turn to the right.
- The footwork is toe, heel, toe.
- There is no rise.
- The timing is quick (beat 5).

Step 4

- Facing LOD, step forward with the right foot in CBMP (8.5*b*).
- Continue to turn right.
- The footwork is heel.
- There is no rise.
- The timing is quick (beat 6).

Lady's Part

Step 1

- Facing DC and moving LOD, step side with the right foot in promenade position.
- There is no turn.
- The footwork is heel.
- There is no rise.
- The timing is slow (beats 1 and 2).

Step 2

- Pointing LOD, step forward and across in CBMP and promenade position with the left foot.
- There is an eighth turn to the right.
- The footwork is heel.
- There is no rise.
- The timing is slow (beats 3 and 4).

Step 3

- Facing LOD, step forward with the right foot (8.5*a*) and end backing LOD.
- There is half a turn to the right.
- The footwork is heel, toe, heel.
- There is no rise.
- The timing is quick (beat 5).

Step 4

- Backing LOD step to the side and slightly back with the left foot (8.5*b*), pivoting to end facing LOD.
- There is three-eighths turn to the right.
- The footwork is toe, heel.
- There is no rise.
- The timing is quick (beat 6).

(continued)

Promenade Pivot　*(continued)*

Gentleman's Part	Lady's Part

Step 5

- Facing DW and moving LOD, step side with the left foot in promenade position (8.5c).
- There is an eighth turn to the right between steps 4 and 5.
- The footwork is heel.
- There is no rise.
- The timing is slow (beats 7 and 8).

Step 6

- Facing DW and moving LOD, step forward and across in CBMP and promenade position with the right foot.
- Continue to turn to the right.
- The footwork is heel, toe.
- There is a slight rise at the end of this step.
- The timing is slow (beats 1 and 2).

Step 7

- Facing wall, step side with the left foot.
- There is an eighth turn to the right between steps 6 and 7.
- The footwork is toe, heel.
- The rise is up, then lower at the end of this step.
- The timing is quick (beat 3).

Step 8

- Facing wall, close the right foot to the left foot.
- There is no turn.
- The footwork is toe, heel.
- Stay down on this step.
- The timing is quick (beat 4).

Step 5

- Facing DC and moving LOD, step side with the right foot in promenade position (8.5c).
- There is no turn.
- The footwork is heel.
- There is no rise.
- The timing is slow (beats 7 and 8).

Step 6

- Facing DC and moving LOD, step forward and across in promenade position with the left foot.
- Start to turn to the left.
- The footwork is heel, toe.
- There is a slight rise at the end of this step.
- The timing is slow (beats 1 and 2).

Step 7

- Backing wall, step side with the right foot.
- There is an eighth turn to the left between steps 6 and 7.
- The footwork is toe, heel.
- The rise is up, then lower at the end of this step.
- The timing is quick (beat 3).

Step 8

- Backing wall, close the left foot to the right foot.
- There is no turn.
- The footwork is toe, heel.
- Stay down on this step.
- The timing is quick (beat 4).

Figure 8.5 Promenade pivot: steps *(a)* 3, *(b)* 4, and *(c)* 5.

Practice Combination

Turning basic—facing DW

Grapevine—facing DW

Turning basic—facing DW

Left turn—facing DW and turning a quarter to end facing DW of new LOD

Promenade pivot—moving along new LOD

Promenade

Left turn—facing wall and turning one-eighth to end facing DW

Grapevine—facing DW

Turning basic—facing DW

OPEN LEFT TURN

This intermediate step is the same as the open left turn in waltz. It should only be used when there is a large dance floor and when both partners have a good understanding of the basic elements of dancing and partnering, such as amount of turn, alignments, and dance position. As with the intermediate step patterns for waltz, these intermediate patterns should not be mixed with the basic patterns.

See this technique demonstrated on the DVD

The feet will not come together at the end of the open left turn, so it moves fluidly around the floor. Note that there is a right outside position on steps 3 and 6. Outside position applies only to the lower body from the middle of the thigh down to the foot; the bodies remain in closed dance position. The correct amount of turn enables the bodies to stay in dance position.

Gentleman's Part

Step 1

- Facing DC, step forward with the left foot.
- Start turning to the left.
- The footwork is heel, toe.
- Rise at the end of this step.
- There is no sway.
- The timing is slow (beats 1 and 2).

Step 2

- Backing DW, step side with the right foot.
- There is a quarter turn to the left between steps 1 and 2.
- The footwork is toe.
- The rise is up.
- Sway to the left.
- The timing is quick (beat 3).

Step 3

- Backing LOD, step back with the left foot in CBMP.
- There is an eighth turn to the left between steps 2 and 3.
- The footwork is toe, heel.
- Up and then lower to a flat foot at the end of the step.
- Sway to the left.
- The timing is quick (beat 4).

Lady's Part

Step 1

- Backing DC, step back with the right foot.
- Start turning to the left.
- The footwork is toe, heel.
- Rise through the body at the end of this step with no foot rise.
- There is no sway.
- The timing is slow (beats 1 and 2).

Step 2

- Pointing LOD, step side and slightly forward with the left foot.
- There is three-eighths turn to the left between steps 1 and 2.
- The footwork is toe.
- The rise is up.
- Sway to the right.
- The timing is quick (beat 3).

Step 3

- Facing LOD, step forward with the right foot in CBMP and outside position.
- The footwork is toe, heel.
- Up and then lower to a flat foot at the end of the step.
- Sway to the right.
- The timing is quick (beat 4).

Step 4

- Backing LOD, step back with the right foot.
- Start turning to the left.
- The footwork is toe, heel.
- Rise through the body at the end of this step with no foot rise.
- There is no sway.
- The timing is slow (beats 5 and 6).

Step 5

- Pointing DW, step side and slightly forward with the left foot.
- There is three-eighths turn to the left between steps 4 and 5.
- The footwork is toe.
- The rise is up.
- Sway to the right.
- The timing is quick (beat 7).

Step 6

- Facing DW, step forward with the right foot in CBMP and outside position.
- The footwork is toe, heel.
- Up and then lower to a flat foot at the end of the step.
- Sway to the right.
- The timing is quick (beat 8).

Step 4

- Facing LOD, step forward with the left foot.
- Start turning to the left.
- The footwork is heel, toe.
- Rise at the end of this step.
- There is no sway.
- The timing is slow (beats 5 and 6).

Step 5

- Backing wall, step side with the right foot.
- There is a quarter turn to the left between steps 4 and 5.
- The footwork is toe, heel.
- The rise is up.
- Sway to the left.
- The timing is quick (beat 7).

Step 6

- Backing DW, step back with the left foot in CBMP.
- There is an eighth turn to the left between steps 5 and 6.
- The footwork is toe, heel.
- Up with no foot rise.
- Sway to the left.
- The timing is quick (beat 8).

RUNNING STEPS

See this technique
demonstrated on
the DVD
Combined with the open left turn, this pattern keeps you moving around the line of dance. However, a large dance floor is needed because there will be more movement in these intermediate patterns than in the basic patterns. The step pattern for running steps is described starting and ending on the line of dance (LOD), but can also be danced at other alignments, such as beginning diagonal wall (DW) and ending DW. And it can curve slightly to the left during steps 1, 2, and 3, so it can begin DW and end LOD or diagonal center (DC), or it can start LOD and end DC.

There is a right outside position on step 6. Remember that outside position applies only to the lower body from the middle of the thigh down to the feet. The bodies remain in closed dance position. The lady's footwork going backward is always toe, heel, even though the man has foot rise.

Gentleman's Part

Step 1

- Facing LOD, step forward with the left foot.
- There is no turn.
- The footwork is heel.
- There is no rise.
- There is no sway.
- The timing is slow (beats 1 and 2).

Step 2

- Facing LOD, step forward with the right foot.
- There is no turn.
- The footwork is heel, toe.
- Rise at the end of this step.
- The sway is left.
- The timing is quick (beat 3).

Step 3

- Facing LOD, step forward with the left foot.
- There is no turn.

Lady's Part

Step 1

- Backing LOD, step back with the right foot.
- There is no turn.
- The footwork is toe, heel.
- There is no rise.
- There is no sway.
- The timing is slow (beats 1 and 2).

Step 2

- Backing LOD, step back with the left foot.
- There is no turn.
- The footwork is toe, heel.
- Rise through the body at the end of this step with no foot rise.
- The sway is right.
- The timing is quick (beat 3).

Step 3

- Backing LOD, step back with the right foot.

- The footwork is toe, heel.
- Up and then lower to a flat foot at the end of this step.
- The sway is left.
- The timing is quick (beat 4).

Step 4
- Facing LOD, step forward with the right foot.
- There is no turn.
- The footwork is heel, toe.
- Rise at the end of this step.
- There is no sway.
- The timing is slow (beats 5 and 6).

Step 5
- Facing LOD, step forward with the left foot.
- There is no turn.
- The footwork is toe.
- The rise is up.
- The sway is right.
- The timing is quick (beat 7).

Step 6
- Facing LOD, step forward with the right foot in CBMP and outside position (8.6).
- There is no turn.
- The footwork is toe, heel.
- Up and then lower to a flat foot at the end of this step.
- The sway is right.
- The timing is quick (beat 8).

- There is no turn.
- The footwork is toe, heel.
- Rise through the body with no foot rise, then lower at the end of the step.
- The sway is right.
- The timing is quick (beat 4).

Step 4
- Backing LOD, step back with the left foot.
- There is no turn.
- The footwork is toe, heel.
- Rise through the body at the end of this step with no foot rise.
- There is no sway.
- The timing is slow (beats 5 and 6).

Step 5
- Backing LOD, step back with the right foot.
- There is no turn.
- The footwork is toe, heel.
- The rise is up through the body with no foot rise.
- The sway is left.
- The timing is quick (beat 7).

Step 6
- Backing LOD, step back with the left foot in CBMP (8.6).
- There is no turn.
- The footwork is toe, heel.
- The rise is up through the body with no foot rise and then lower at the end of this step.
- The sway is left.
- The timing is quick (beat 8).

(continued)

Running Steps　*(continued)*

Figure 8.6　Running steps: step 6.

Basic Foxtrot Step Pattern Combinations

Combination #1

> See this technique demonstrated on the DVD

Two turning basics—facing DW

Two chasses—facing DW

Left turn—facing DW and turning one-eighth to end facing LOD

Two promenades—moving along new LOD

Two left turns—facing wall and turning three-eighths to end facing DW of new LOD

Turning basic—facing DW

Combination #2

Two turning basics—facing DW

Grapevine—facing DW

Left turn—facing DW and turning a quarter to end facing DW of the new LOD (If you can't make a quarter turn, dance two left turn patterns, each turning one-eighth.)

Turning basic—facing DW

Three chasses—facing DW

Left turn—facing DW and turning one-eighth to end facing LOD

Promenade with underarm turn—moving along new LOD

Two chasses—facing wall

Left turn—facing wall and turning one-eighth to end facing DW

Combination #3

Two turning basics—facing DW

Four chasses—facing DW

Grapevine—facing DW

Left turn—facing DW and turning one-eighth to end facing LOD

Promenade pivot—moving along new LOD

Two left turns—facing wall and turning three-eighths to end facing DW of the new LOD

Turning basic—facing DW

Intermediate Foxtrot Step Pattern Combinations

Combination #1

> See this technique demonstrated on the DVD

Open left turn—facing DC

Running steps—facing DW and turning one quarter over steps 1 and 2 to end facing DC

Open left turn—facing DC

Combination #2

Note: This combination includes waltz figures. The open right turn from the waltz is included in this combination. It is danced the same as in the waltz except that you use the timing for the foxtrot of slow, quick, quick instead of 1, 2, 3 as in the waltz.

Open left turn—facing DC

Running steps—facing DW, the first three steps curve to face new LOD and the last three steps continue to curve to face DW of new LOD

Open right turn—facing DW, end facing DC

Running steps—facing DC with no turn to end facing DW of new LOD

9

American Style Viennese Waltz

T he origins of Viennese waltz can be traced back to folk dances in Germany and Austria. The couples rotated on a spot and stayed in very close dance position. Later, the dance developed into a progressive movement, but still remained rotational as it traveled around the dance floor. The right turns were the first turns to be danced. The lady was held on the man's right side because his sword was carried on the left side. It was proper for the man to ask if the lady turned left. If she did, then he danced the left turns. Turning right was called a *natural turn* and turning left a *reverse turn*, and those terms are still used today.

The twirling character of the Viennese waltz is exemplified by the rotation and sweeping movement down the floor and should look effortless. The dance has a look of elegance and high society. There is much more rotation of the bodies in some of the patterns in the Viennese waltz, and the dance moves much faster than the waltz that was covered in chapter 6. The music most associated with the Viennese waltz is classical in style, but some popular songs have been complementary to the musicality of the dance as well. The artist Enya released a beautiful Viennese waltz called "Caribbean Blue" in the 1990s. In the 1998 movie *Practical Magic*, with Sandra Bullock and Nicole Kidman, there was a Viennese waltz called "Amas Veritas." Bryan Adams had a big hit with "Have You Ever Really Loved a Woman," also a Viennese waltz.

The music is written in 3/4 time just like the slow waltz, but the tempo is much quicker. The beats per minute for a slow waltz range from 84 to 128, but for a Viennese waltz the beats per minute can be 162 to 174, a significant difference in the tempo. Authentic Viennese waltz music plays the second beat of each bar a little quicker than a strict time space between each beat. That means that count 2 is slightly closer to count 1 than it is to count 3. It would look something like this: 1-2—3. The difference in the beat value gives the dance a distinctive feeling. Besides being faster than a slow waltz, there is a special vitality to it. Most dancers don't really hear the difference in the timing, but they are aware of a different feel to the music when it is an authentic Viennese waltz. The more contemporary songs listed earlier do not have that authentic feel, but because of the beat and tempo, they can still be used to dance a Viennese waltz. Because of the quick tempo of the Viennese waltz, the rise and fall is shallow and is created by the swinging of the body. There is very little foot rise.

There are not as many step patterns in this chapter as in others because Viennese waltz is a more difficult dance to learn. It is not a beginners' dance because of the very quick tempo. Correct posture and dance position and a very good understanding of how to move the body must be mastered before this dance can be attempted. Because the tempo of the music is much quicker, the first few step patterns in this chapter use hesitations to help in the learning process. Hesitations were also used in the slow waltz. A hesitation is taking a step on count 1 and then holding that position for the next two counts. The next step patterns start the dancers moving and turning their bodies slightly. When comfortable moving to the tempo of the music, the last two patterns, which are the rotational patterns, may be added so that the dance moves around the floor. As a social dance, Viennese waltz uses more basic patterns than the other dances. It stays in dance position most of the time so that the two bodies are able to move comfortably together. There is rarely separation except in the upper levels or in competition or exhibition dancing.

Refer to the discussions of posture and dance position in chapters 4 and 5. The details of footwork and foot position are explained in chapter 4. Sway is explained in chapter 5. The alignments noted in the practice combinations are all written to describe the direction the man faces to begin the step pattern.

Basic Social Viennese Waltz Patterns

Side hesitations
Forward and backward hesitations
Forward change steps—left to right, right to left
Turns—left turn, right turn

SIDE HESITATIONS

This pattern helps dancers feel the speed of the music without having to move very much. As explained earlier, it is a good pattern to practice hearing the tempo of the music, and it also is a good way to begin dancing this dance. It gives the dancers an idea of the tempo before they begin progressive movement. The movement is side to side with a slight pressure on the foot that is closing and is similar to the hesitation steps in the slow waltz. When danced during the actual dance, the figure may be danced at any alignment depending on the preceding figure. It could be used as an evasive step to avoid dance traffic, or in a corner to slow down and regroup if the dancers are getting tired and out of dance position.

See this technique demonstrated on the DVD

Gentleman's Part

Step 1 (Beat 1)
- Facing line of dance (LOD), step side with the left foot.
- Footwork is toe, heel.

Step 2 (Beat 2)
- Facing LOD, close the right foot to the left foot with no weight change.
- Footwork is ball.

Step 3 (Beat 3)
- Facing LOD, hold that position without changing weight.
- Footwork is pressure on ball of right foot.

Step 4 (Beat 1)
- Facing LOD, step side with the right foot.
- Footwork is toe, heel.

Step 5 (Beat 2)
- Facing LOD, close the left foot to the right foot with no weight change.
- Footwork is ball.

Step 6 (Beat 3)
- Facing LOD, hold that position without changing weight.
- Footwork is pressure on ball of left foot.

Lady's Part

Step 1 (Beat 1)
- Backing LOD, step side with the right foot.
- Footwork is toe, heel.

Step 2 (Beat 2)
- Backing LOD, close the left foot to the right foot with no weight change.
- Footwork is ball.

Step 3 (Beat 3)
- Backing LOD, hold that position without changing weight.
- Footwork is pressure on ball of left foot.

Step 4 (Beat 1)
- Backing LOD, step side with the left foot.
- Footwork is toe, heel.

Step 5 (Beat 2)
- Backing LOD, close the right foot to the left foot with no weight change.
- Footwork is ball.

Step 6 (Beat 3)
- Backing LOD, hold that position without changing weight.
- Footwork is pressure on ball of right foot.

FORWARD AND BACKWARD HESITATIONS

See this technique demonstrated on the DVD

This pattern is danced similarly to the side hesitation pattern, but it moves forward and back. It is used for the same purposes as the side hesitations—it is just a variation. In hesitations, both side and forward and backward, there is no sway. The hesitations are danced with a slight body rise, but no foot rise. There is no turn during the hesitations, but they may be danced at different alignments, depending on the end alignment of the preceding figure. When dancing a hesitation, keep ankle, knee, and hip joints relaxed so you can move easily from foot to foot. Keep pressure on the closing foot for better balance, but do not put all your weight on it.

Gentleman's Part

Step 1 (Beat 1)
- Facing LOD, step forward with the left foot.
- Footwork is heel.

Step 2 (Beat 2)
- Facing LOD, close the right foot to the left foot with no weight change.
- Footwork is ball.

Step 3 (Beat 3)
- Facing LOD, hold that position without changing weight.
- Footwork is pressure on ball of right foot.

Step 4 (Beat 1)
- Backing against LOD, step back with the right foot.
- Footwork is toe, heel.

Step 5 (Beat 2)
- Backing against LOD, close the left foot to the right foot with no weight change.
- Footwork is ball.

Step 6 (Beat 3)
- Backing against LOD, hold that position without changing weight.
- Footwork is pressure on ball of left foot.

Lady's Part

Step 1 (Beat 1)
- Backing LOD, step back with the right foot.
- Footwork is toe, heel.

Step 2 (Beat 2)
- Backing LOD, close the left foot to the right foot with no weight change.
- Footwork is ball.

Step 3 (Beat 3)
- Backing LOD, hold that position without changing weight.
- Footwork is pressure on ball of left foot.

Step 4 (Beat 1)
- Facing against LOD, step forward with the left foot.
- Footwork is heel.

Step 5 (Beat 2)
- Facing against LOD, close the right foot to the left foot with no weight change.
- Footwork is ball.

Step 6 (Beat 3)
- Facing against LOD, hold that position without changing weight.
- Footwork is pressure on ball of right foot.

Practice Combination

Two side hesitations
Two forward and backward hesitations

FORWARD CHANGE STEP

The forward change steps in Viennese waltz are mainly used between the left and right turns to get dancers on the correct foot for the next pattern. For example: there is a forward change step left to right after a left turn if the next step pattern will be a right turn, and there is a forward change step right to left after the right turn if the next step pattern will be a left turn. The pattern is similar to the forward progressive basic in slow waltz and can also be used to move forward down the line of dance. Other alignments can be used, which are determined by the ending alignment of the preceding figure. No amount of turn is listed, but there is a slight body turn to the left on the left to right pattern and to the right on the right to left pattern. This book describes the alignments of both as starting facing line of dance, but advanced dancers begin the forward change step left to right facing diagonal center (DC) and the forward change step right to left facing diagonal wall (DW). On the DVD, the forward change steps are demonstrated using the diagonal alignments.

See this technique demonstrated on the DVD

Forward Change Step: Left to Right

Gentleman's Part

Step 1 (Beat 1)
- Facing LOD, step forward with the left foot.
- Footwork is heel, toe.
- There is no sway.

Step 2 (Beat 2)
- Facing LOD, step diagonally forward with the right foot.
- Footwork is toe.
- There is sway to the left.

Lady's Part

Step 1 (Beat 1)
- Backing LOD, step back with the right foot.
- Footwork is toe, heel.
- There is no sway.

Step 2 (Beat 2)
- Backing LOD, step diagonally back with the left foot.
- Footwork is toe.
- There is sway to the right.

Step 3 (Beat 3)

- Facing LOD, close the left foot to the right foot.
- Footwork is toe, heel.
- There is sway to the left.

Step 3 (Beat 3)

- Backing LOD, close the right foot to the left foot.
- Footwork is toe, heel.
- There is sway to the right.

Forward Change Step: Right to Left

See this technique demonstrated on the DVD

Gentleman's Part

Step 1 (Beat 1)

- Facing LOD, step forward with the right foot.
- Footwork is heel, toe.
- There is no sway.

Step 2 (Beat 2)

- Facing LOD, step diagonally forward with the left foot.
- Footwork is toe.
- There is sway to the right.

Step 3 (Beat 3)

- Facing LOD, close the right foot to the left foot.
- Footwork is toe, heel.
- There is sway to the right.

Lady's Part

Step 1 (Beat 1)

- Backing LOD, step back with the left foot.
- Footwork is toe, heel.
- There is no sway.

Step 2 (Beat 2)

- Backing LOD, step diagonally back with the right foot.
- Footwork is toe.
- The sway is to the left.

Step 3 (Beat 3)

- Backing LOD, close the left foot to the right foot.
- Footwork is toe, heel.
- The sway is to the left.

Practice Combination

Two side hesitations—facing LOD

Forward change step left to right—facing LOD

Forward change step right to left—facing LOD

Two forward and backward hesitations—facing LOD

Forward change step left to right—facing LOD

Forward change step right to left—facing LOD

TURNS

The left and right turns are the patterns that move the dance around the floor and create the look of the dance, which is rotational. In the waltz, left turns always started facing DC and right turns facing DW. But because of the speed of the Viennese waltz, each measure of 1, 2, 3 turns four-eighths (or half) of a turn instead of three-eighths of a turn, so the alignments are different. This book describes the alignments of both as starting along the line of dance, but advanced dancers begin the left turns DW, and the right turns DC. On the DVD, left and right turns are demonstrated facing DW and DC, respectively.

For beginners, it is easier to dance the left turns down the line of dance and the right turns around the corners of the room. Because of dance position—the woman slightly offset to the right of the man—the amount of turn naturally increases slightly as the left turns are danced and decreases slightly as the right turns are danced. As the dancers become more advanced and comfortable with the amount of turn, the turns may be interchanged: left turns danced around the corners of the room and right turns down the line of dance.

The man and the woman must feel that when they do the forward half of the pattern, they are moving on a straight line toward their partner. The person going back turns off the line. Because of the tempo of the music and the amount of turn, dance position must be maintained. When the man closes his feet during the back half of the left and right turns, his closing foot has to be flat, and when the woman closes her feet on the back half of turns, her closing foot is almost flat.

See this technique demonstrated on the DVD ## Left Turn

Gentleman's Part

Step 1 (Beat 1)
- Facing LOD, step forward with the left foot.
- Start to turn left.
- The footwork is heel, toe.
- There is no sway.

Lady's Part

Step 1 (Beat 1)
- Backing LOD, step back and slightly side with the right foot, and the toe turned in.
- Start to turn left.
- The footwork is toe, heel.
- There is no sway.

Step 2 (Beat 2)
- Backing wall, step side with the right foot.
- There is a quarter turn between steps 1 and 2.
- Footwork is toe.
- The sway is to the left.

Step 3 (Beat 3)
- Backing LOD, cross the left foot in front of the right foot (9.1*a*).
- There is another quarter turn between steps 2 and 3.
- The footwork is toe, heel.
- The sway is to the left.

Step 4 (Beat 1)
- Backing LOD, step back and slightly side with the right foot, and the toe turned in.
- Start to turn left.
- The footwork is toe, heel.
- There is no sway.

Step 5 (Beat 2)
- Pointing LOD, step side with the left foot.
- There is almost three-eighths turn to the left between steps 4 and 5, with less body turn.
- The footwork is toe.
- The sway is to the right.

Step 6 (Beat 3)
- Facing LOD, close the right foot to the left foot as the body turn is completed (9.1*b*).
- There is about an eighth turn between steps 5 and 6.
- Footwork is flat.
- The sway is to the right.

Step 2 (Beat 2)
- Pointing almost LOD, step side with left foot.
- There is about three-eighths turn to the left between steps 1 and 2 with less body turn.
- The footwork is toe.
- The sway is to the right.

Step 3 (Beat 3)
- Facing LOD, close the right foot to the left foot as the body turn is completed (9.1*a*).
- There is about an eighth turn to the left between steps 2 and 3.
- The footwork is toe, heel, but it is almost flat.
- The sway is to the right.

Step 4 (Beat 1)
- Facing LOD, step forward with the left foot.
- Start to turn left.
- The footwork is heel, toe.
- There is no sway.

Step 5 (Beat 2)
- Backing wall, step side and slightly back with the right foot.
- There is a quarter turn to the left between steps 4 and 5.
- The footwork is toe.
- The sway is to the left.

Step 6 (Beat 3)
- Backing LOD, cross the left foot in front of the right foot (9.1*b*).
- There is about a quarter turn to the left between steps 5 and 6.
- The footwork is toe, heel.
- The sway is to the left.

(continued)

Left Turn   *(continued)*

Figure 9.1   Left turn: steps *(a)* 3 and *(b)* 6.

See this technique demonstrated on the DVD

Right Turn

Gentleman's Part

Step 1 (Beat 1)

- Facing LOD, step forward with the right foot.
- Start to turn right.
- The footwork is heel, toe.
- There is no sway.

Step 2 (Beat 2)

- Backing DC, step side with the left foot.
- There is three-eighths turn to the right between steps 1 and 2.
- The footwork is toe.
- The sway is to the right.

Lady's Part

Step 1 (Beat 1)

- Backing LOD, step back and slightly side with the left foot, and the toe turned in.
- Start to turn right.
- The footwork is toe, heel.
- There is no sway.

Step 2 (Beat 2)

- Pointing LOD, step side with the right foot.
- There is a half turn to the right between steps 1 and 2, but the body turn is less.
- The footwork is toe.
- The sway is to the left.

Step 3 (Beat 3)

- Backing LOD, close the right foot to the left foot.
- There is an eighth turn to the right between steps 2 and 3.
- The footwork is toe, heel.
- The sway is to the right.

Step 4 (Beat 1)

- Backing LOD, step back and slightly side with the left foot, and the toe turned in.
- Start to turn right.
- The footwork is toe, heel.
- There is no sway.

Step 5 (Beat 2)

- Pointing LOD, step side with the right foot.
- There is a half turn to the right between steps 4 and 5, but the body turn is less.
- The footwork is toe.
- The sway is to the left.

Step 6 (Beat 3)

- Facing LOD, close the left foot to the right foot.
- The body will complete the turn between steps 5 and 6.
- The footwork is flat.
- The sway is to the left.

Step 3 (Beat 3)

- Facing LOD, close the left foot to the right foot.
- The body will complete the turn between steps 2 and 3.
- The footwork is toe, heel, but it is almost flat.
- The sway is to the left.

Step 4 (Beat 1)

- Facing LOD, step forward with the right foot.
- Start to turn right.
- The footwork is heel, toe.
- There is no sway.

Step 5 (Beat 2)

- Backing DC, step side with the left foot.
- There is three-eighths turn to the right between steps 4 and 5.
- The footwork is toe.
- The sway is to the right.

Step 6 (Beat 3)

- Backing LOD, close the right foot to the left foot.
- There is an eighth turn to the right between steps 5 and 6.
- The footwork is toe, heel.
- The sway is to the right.

Viennese Waltz Step Pattern Combinations

Combination #1

Two side hesitations—facing DW

Two left turns—facing DW

Two forward and backward hesitations—facing DW

Two left turns—facing DW

> See this technique demonstrated on the DVD

Combination #2

Two side hesitations—facing DC

Forward change step left to right—facing DC

Two right turns—facing DC

Forward change step right to left—facing DC

Two forward and backward hesitations—facing DC

Side hesitations—facing DC

Combination #3

Two side hesitations—facing DW

Two left turns—facing DW

Forward change step left to right—facing DW and turning a quarter to face DW of new LOD

Three right turns—facing DW and turning first a total of three-quarters to end facing DC, then facing DC and turning twice around the corner, on second one to face DW of new LOD

Forward change step right to left—facing DW

PART

III

Ballroom Dancing on Your Own

CHAPTER 10

Surviving the Social Dance Floor

*I*t's time to step out from practicing in your kitchen and start dancing in public. This chapter will help you get ready for your first time out on the dance floor. Wearing dance attire and shoes that are comfortable and make you feel good is an important aspect of dancing. If you look like a dancer, you will start to feel like a dancer. Suggestions for dance attire and shoes to help you to look your best are covered in this chapter. Another important topic, dance etiquette, is discussed. Social dancing is a whole new world, and if you know the basic principles, moving into that world will be much easier. Traveling around the dance floor with ease and fluidity is another hurdle that the social dancer must face. We discuss this topic a little more in this chapter. Just being aware of these aspects will help make your first step on the dance floor easy and enjoyable.

ATTIRE AND FOOTWEAR

While getting started on this new hobby, certain accessories and articles of clothing will make you more comfortable. The way to dress depends on what kind of dance function you are attending. Regardless of the kind of function, women usually feel more like a dancer in a skirt or dress than in a pants outfit. Ballroom dancing implies romance. A flowing dress is more feminine than pants and adds to the romantic feeling of the dancing and the music. The ballroom dances have a smooth, flowing quality. A skirt not only imparts that same quality to the viewer, but more important, to the dancer. Simply put, if you feel elegant, you will dance in an elegant manner. Depending on the formality of the affair, pants outfits for ladies may be acceptable, of course, but when talking about conveying a desired quality, skirts are the best choice.

If you are attending a casual dance, such as a dance at a club that has monthly dances or at a ballroom dance studio's practice parties, a nice full skirt or dress is appropriate for the woman. The length of the skirt can be anywhere from just below the knee to hitting the top of the ankle bone. Many dance Web

sites sell skirts made specifically for ballroom dancing,
and there are blouses and
tops to go with them. These
skirts have a lot of material,
so they flow as the dancer
moves. Various fabrics and
colors are used, but something fairly lightweight yet
durable is the norm. At these
types of casual dances, men
usually wear dress pants and a
comfortable collared shirt that
buttons, or even a polo shirt
and khakis. Think business
casual. Sometimes men might
also choose to wear a tie or a
sport coat or both, but these
are usually not necessary unless
the man wants to feel a little
more dressed up for the evening.
Jeans, shorts, and T-shirts are
usually too casual and don't
impart the elegant feeling of the
music and the dancing. When
you are in baggy shorts and a T-
shirt, you feel like lounging. But
when you are in something a little

A dark suit and a smart cocktail dress are appropriate
attire for semiformal functions and allow comfortable, easy movement.

more tailored, your body will respond with better posture, preparing you for
dancing properly. Even at a casual event, it's still possible to feel elegant and
properly dressed for dancing without compromising comfort.

The terms *formal*, *semiformal*, and *informal* have evolved through the years
as social dress standards have relaxed. Formal used to mean white bow tie
and tails, and semiformal meant black bow tie and tuxedo. It still holds true
today that if the dance is a traditional formal affair, such as a royal wedding,
state dinner, or presidential inauguration, the men wear a white bow tie and
black tails. The majority of dancers will never attend anything like that, but
there are some ballroom dances and social functions that still adhere to this
tradition, such as some debutante cotillions or high-society events. Today,
if an event calls for traditional white tie and tails, the invitation will usually
read "white tie," or occasionally "full evening dress." In this case, white tie
and tails are expected. If semiformal attire is called for, the invitation will usually read "black tie." For a black-tie affair, a black tuxedo with a black bow
tie is appropriate. It can get confusing: Sometimes the word *formal* is used
to mean black tie. A good rule of thumb is, that unless it is an extremely or

unusually important event (like those mentioned earlier for white tie), black tie is appropriate for formal events. And remember, with tails, black ties are never worn, only white. If an invitation reads *semiformal*, in today's language that usually means a dark suit and tie for the gentlemen. Tuxedos would be fine, but are not required unless black tie is stated. *Informal* on an invitation is a step above casual. A suit and tie are appropriate. For the serious male dancer, there are specially made suits and tuxedos for dancing that are more comfortable than a standard tuxedo.

The descriptive terms used to identify proper attire for an event (formal, semiformal, white tie, black tie, and so on) are taken from the man's dress. With women's attire, there is less black and white, so to speak, and more shades of gray. However, if an event is *traditional* formal, or "white tie," women are expected to be in ball gowns. A ball gown, in traditional terms, is a dress with a full skirt that reaches at least to the ankles. But if it is too long, there may be problems while dancing. The heel of the woman's shoe can get caught in it or she may even trip over it. Although longer dresses and dresses with trains (material that drags along the floor behind the dress) may be appropriate for white-tie affairs, if dancing is to be involved, avoid those types of dresses. Instead, opt for a ball gown that reaches the top of the ankle bone, which allows for more comfortable dancing and prevents potential accidents while still being appropriate for a white-tie event. The materials used for ball gowns are luxurious, such as silk, satin, chiffon, velvet, and lace, and any color is acceptable.

Traditionally, at a black-tie event, women wear evening gowns. An evening gown is a long, flowing dress ranging in length from tea length (two inches [five centimeters] above the ankle) to full length. At a semiformal affair, a range of dress types and skirt lengths are appropriate. In today's fashion, if the event is not specifically black tie (men in tuxedos), but semiformal (men in dark suits or tuxedos), women may wear anything from an evening gown to a cocktail dress. A cocktail dress is usually a shorter dress, anywhere from just above the knee to tea length. In any event, if dancing is expected during the evening, it's important that the dress or skirt be comfortable and easy to move in. A tight skirt constricts the body's ability to move with ease. Fabrics for formal and semiformal affairs can be anything as long as they are comfortable and easy to dance in, and colors are open to whatever the woman desires.

The norm today is traditional formal wear as a starting point for creative formal wear—the attire we see at weddings, proms, and ballroom dances. Almost anything goes—red, purple, or green bow ties or even no tie at all are all widely worn variations on the traditional black tie with a tuxedo. And as we have seen, standards are less stringent when it comes to attire for the ladies. Cocktail dresses are becoming dressier than in the past and more acceptable even at formal events. For more information on practice wear and performance attire for both men and women, see the resources section at the end of the book.

To summarize, at a white-tie event, men in white tie and tails and ladies in ball gowns is expected and required. At black-tie events, men are in black tie and black tuxedos, and women are in anything from cocktail dresses to evening gowns. At formal events that are not specifically black tie, men wear tuxedos or dark suits and women wear the same as at black-tie events. Casual events call for business casual for men, and skirts or dresses for women (cocktail length to just above the ankle bone). For most dance functions you will attend, such as weekly or monthly studio dances, casual attire is in order. For most ballroom functions, such as dance studio holiday parties or dance club special events, semiformal attire is acceptable unless otherwise specified.

A good pair of dance shoes is also important. Professionally made dance shoes give the right kind of support for dancing. They have special suede (chrome leather) soles for easier movement, and the soles are flexible so the dancer can feel the floor. There are various styles and types of ladies shoes. Some have T-straps, some are pumps, and others even have ankle straps (see figure 10.1). They are made of leather or satin and come in a variety of colors. They can even sparkle. Many women like beige shoes the best, because they go with almost any outfit. And if you decide to go on further with your dancing and perhaps get into competition or exhibition dancing, shoes in a flesh tone are best as they seem to extend the leg line, giving the dance a more pleasing appearance. For ballroom dancing, shoes with a closed toe are best. The typical heel height is two and a half inches (6.3 centimeters), but lower heels can be found if needed. Ballroom shoes should fit snuggly but not so tight that they are painful. The foot should not be able to move around in the shoe. When you are looking for shoes, remember that leather and satin both stretch, so if they are a little loose to start with, they will get even looser.

Men don't have nearly the number of choices that women have. The most popular choices are black leather or black patent leather (see figure 10.2), but men's shoes also come in a few other colors and materials. Brown, tan, or spectator shoes (two-tone shoes, usually black and white, similar in appearance

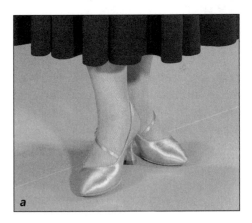
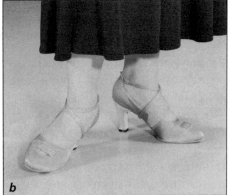

Figure 10.1 Examples of two types of women's dance shoes.

Figure 10.2 A pair of men's dance shoes.

to saddle shoes) are available, as well as all-suede shoes or a combination of leather types. Whatever the style, they should fit snuggly, which means the foot should not be able to move around in the shoe, just like for the women's shoes.

Because of the special suede sole of professionally made dance shoes, they rarely (if ever) should be worn outdoors. Water will damage the soles, as will grass and soil. Some accessories you may want to invest in to protect your dance shoes and make them last longer are a bag to carry them in to dances and a shoe brush. A shoe brush is for the suede sole of ballroom shoes; it's made of stiff, metal bristles and is used to brush accumulated floor wax and other debris from the soles, allowing the shoes to maintain the proper traction on the dance floor and not become too slippery or sticky. Look in the resources section for more information on shoes and accessories.

If you are just beginning and not yet sure if you want to invest in specially made ballroom shoes, there are a few things to consider on footwear. Avoid sneakers and other rubber-soled shoes because they will not allow the foot to move properly on the floor. A pair of hard-soled shoes will be fine to start with, such as a dress oxford for men or a shoe with some sort of heel for women. You won't have the same sort of flexibility and feeling as you will from shoes made specifically for ballroom dancing, but those are okay to start with. Later, if you decide that dancing is something you want to pursue further, you will want to invest in at least one pair of dance shoes.

BALLROOM ETIQUETTE

Proper etiquette and politeness are essential qualities that everyone needs in order to be successful in life. The attitude you show to the people around you, friends and strangers, determines how they perceive you. Nowhere is that more evident than on the social dance floor. Potential dance partners decide if they want to dance with you by your attitude and manners. There are some rules of etiquette that should not be broken at a social dance. These basic practices will make you one of the most sought-after dance partners at the dance and will help to ensure an enjoyable event and a safe dance environment. Whether you have a regular dance partner or you are dancing with a variety of partners, the same rules of etiquette and partnering apply.

Grooming is important at social dances. As dancers, we get in closer proximity to others than we generally do in daily life, so personal grooming is of the utmost importance. Being freshly showered and well dressed will also do wonders for your confidence. Take the time to consider the details of appearance—shaved, clothes pressed, makeup and hair in place. Brush your teeth and use baby powder and deodorant as required. Light colognes and perfumes are great, but avoid very strong or overpowering scents. If you tend to perspire, a handkerchief to dab perspiration from your brow between dances is a good idea. And be prepared to have a good time; no one wants to dance with someone who is not smiling and at ease!

Sometimes it's easier to be polite to a stranger than to your own significant other. But to dance well together there must be mutual respect and confidence between yourself and your partner. As we discussed in chapter 5, the element of partnering is important for two people dancing together. The man should never be rough and try to force his partner to do something. He should not hold her too closely either. Probably the longer two people dance together the closer they will hold their bodies to each other. That's only natural; as a person's comfort level with someone increases, he or she will be more comfortable being closer together. The ultimate goal is to just lightly touch bodies. If someone does not want to get too close, don't force him or her. Be aware of each other's personal space and comfort level. The woman should always move her own body and not lay her weight on the man. And of course she should always let the man decide what steps they are going to do and the timing of the steps. Ladies must remember that the man is the leader on the dance floor, and she must not do what is sometimes referred to as *back leading*. This is when the lady essentially takes over leading the step by manipulating or guiding the man. Sometimes ladies think this is helping the beginning dancer, but it really doesn't serve him well. He can't learn to lead confidently if he is not given the opportunity. These principles are the same whether you are dancing with a stranger, a friend, or your regular dance partner.

Young gentlemen are earnestly advised not to limit their conversation to remarks on the weather and the heat of the room. It is, to a certain extent, incumbent on them to do something more than dance when they invite a lady to join in a quadrille. If it be only upon the news of the day, a gentleman should be able to offer at least three or four observations to his partner in the course of a long half-hour.

From Mixing in Society: A Complete Manual of Manners *by the Right Hon. Countess of **** (London and New York: George Routledge & Sons, 1860)*

Although dancing with a variety of partners can be beneficial, having a regular dance partner also has benefits. When two people dance together often, they start to think and move in harmony, and being in a partnership gives you someone to practice with. But even if you have a regular dance partner, dancing with a variety of partners will help you learn how to respond to different people.

Don't be afraid of dancing with people who are more advanced than you are. You can benefit from feeling the way they move. If you feel daunted and are afraid that you won't know the steps they are leading, you can kindly let them know that you are a beginner and apologize for not knowing the more advanced steps. Be gracious, and they will certainly understand and hopefully will dance steps you are more familiar with. Everyone will feel different to dance with, so experiencing those differences will help the learning process by making you a stronger partner.

If you don't have a regular partner that you've been learning with, then you may have some added difficulties. The men do have the advantage, because the man decides what step pattern he's going to do, the timing, and the direction—the leading. So for him, it is somewhat easier to dance with a variety of partners. The lady, on the other hand, has no control of those things, so she is at the mercy of the man. His dance knowledge may be completely different from hers. That is why it's important for her to know how to move her own body so she can respond to whatever the man decides to do. It is good form for the more experienced partner to dance to the level of the less experienced partner. When dancing with a partner for the first time, men should start with simpler patterns, then slowly work up to more advanced patterns if the lady responds well. Ladies should not try to outdance or show off for a less experienced partner; it may confuse him. He may think he has made a mistake if you do something he has not led.

There will always be times when the man will forget some of the step patterns. When that happens he should just try to stay relaxed and dance the patterns that he does remember. If he doesn't get too nervous about it, the memory should return. If he fails to remember it that night, it's okay too; he should just practice it a little more before the next dance. Women shouldn't try to teach the man what he has forgotten. It's his responsibility to decide which step patterns he does and hers to respond to that. If the woman has a hard time responding to the step pattern that the man is doing, then he should move on to another pattern. The dance should be a fun experience. It's important to remember that everyone is doing his or her best and no one makes a mistake or forgets a pattern on purpose.

One of the most important rules, and unfortunately the most broken rule, is to never criticize or teach your partner. No one wants to be told what to do when actually at the dance. If your regular partner does that, then you should discuss it and find ways to talk with each other about the dancing without either of you getting critical of the other. When a stranger or someone you've met at a dance a few times criticizes you, it can be even more hurtful. Everyone handles criticism in their own way, depending on their personality and the situation. If a stranger criticizes you, it really says more about that person than it says about your dancing. If you can, just stay polite and thank the person, but you may choose not to dance with that person again. If the person asks you why you won't dance with him or her, then truthfully and calmly explain that you came to the dance to have a good time, not to be criticized or taught. Eventually, he or she will learn that treating partners with courtesy and respect will provide more dancing opportunities. There are very few dancers who are really rude; the men and women who criticize usually think their comments and teaching are helpful.

Asking someone to dance is a challenge for most people. Ballroom dancing is a new social situation for many people, and if they have never asked someone for a dance, it may seem daunting at first. It used to be just the man's problem, but now more and more women are doing the asking. So gentlemen, don't be shocked if a lady asks you to dance. When asking someone to dance, don't wave or yell from across the room. Not only is it rude, but several people may think you are asking them, and it would be awkward to tell them the invitation is for someone else. When asking for a dance, walk up to the person, make eye contact, and offer your hand. Always ask politely—for example, "Would you like to dance?" or, "This is such a great song, will you dance with me?" Another way to invite someone to dance is, "I love the foxtrot (waltz, and so on). Would you do me the honor?" or simply, "Care to dance?" The one being asked should also reply politely by saying something like, "I would love to," or, "That sounds like fun," or simply, "Of course." When asking or responding, show some excitement and gratitude; no one wants to feel like dancing with them is a punishment. No matter who did the asking, it is customary for the gentleman to take the lady's hand and escort her onto the dance floor, avoiding couples who are already dancing by walking around the perimeter of the floor, not cutting through dance traffic. If someone turns you down, don't take it personally. Sometimes there are good reasons. The person might be insecure about dancing, and that particular dance may be one that he or she doesn't feel confident with or simply doesn't know. Or the person might just need a break from dancing for a couple of songs.

When turning someone down for a dance, do it politely and give a reason; it might have taken a lot of courage for the person to ask. Ways to turn someone down are: "Thank you, but I need to sit this one out, maybe later." "Thank you, but I don't know this dance." "Thank you, but I really want to watch a specific couple dance this dance." "Thank you, but I promised this dance to someone else." Always say thank you. You want to be known as a courteous and polite dancer. And don't lie. If you say you promised this dance to Mr. Brown, you had better dance with Mr. Brown. If you decline a dance because you want to sit this one out for whatever reason, then you must turn down all subsequent invitations for that song. Lies can catch up with you, and you want to be known as an honest person. Step into that other person's shoes for that moment. Turning down dances is generally not a good thing to do. If you're always turning down partners, pretty soon you'll stop getting asked. In the beginning, it is hard to go out and dance with strangers, but the sooner you jump in, the better it will be for your confidence and ultimately for your dancing. The more people you dance with, the more experiences you will have.

You learn something from all those experiences. You'll develop a deeper pool of knowledge that you can draw from when you're in an awkward situation dancing or dealing with various partners.

> **A**ny lady refusing to dance with a gentleman, if disengaged, will be under the penalty of not joining the next two dances.
>
> *From* A Pocket Companion to French and English Dancing *by G.M.S. Chivers*
> *(London: T. Denham, 1821)*

Another potentially awkward situation is when someone asks your significant other (husband, wife, girlfriend, and so on) to dance. At dance parties held by dance studios and social dance clubs, this often happens. Don't think of it as a singles party where people are looking for a date or romantic involvement. Even married couples enjoy dancing with others. Don't be put off by it; it is just dancing, and you and your significant other will both benefit from dancing with others. In fact, the weekly dances at dance studios are often called practice parties; people are there to practice dancing and to mingle with other dancers.

Sometimes it's difficult to tell what dance to do with the music that is being played. Some music played at nightclubs or weddings isn't really danceable by traditional ballroom standards. If you can't figure it out on your own, then look around and see what other dancers are dancing. Or, if you feel comfortable, ask someone at the dance. You might let the person know you are a beginner, and say something to the effect of, "I'm just starting out, and I can't identify this music. What dance do you do to this?" Then, after the person tells you, thank him or her and perhaps ask the person to dance with you. Before the next dance party, look back over chapter 3 and listen to different types of music to get a feel for it. If you are having a lot of trouble with music identification, try to find someone who understands it to help you with it before the next dance.

After each dance, it is customary to applaud the orchestra. If the music is prerecorded, applauding is not necessary. Thank your partner for the dance. As a side note, when your partner thanks you after a dance, the proper response is, "Thank you," not, "You're welcome!" The reply is not for a favor, but out of courtesy. If you enjoyed the dance, let your partner know. A compliment such as, "You led/followed that grapevine beautifully," or, "You are so easy to dance with" is always nice to hear, especially if you are dancing with someone who may lack confidence. After the dance, it is customary for the gentleman to escort the lady back to her seat. This may not be practical in a large or crowded venue, but use your best judgment. Also, the dance floor is exactly for that—dancing. After a dance has finished, leave the floor unless you plan to dance to the next song with the same partner. If you stand on the floor conversing, you are taking up space that others could be using for dancing. If you want to converse with that particular dance partner further, take the conversation off the dance floor.

STEPPING OUT ON THE DANCE FLOOR

The most important thing to remember is that the learning experience is not over before the first public dance appearance; it's really just beginning. The experience of practicing the dance steps alone or even with a partner is nothing like maneuvering around a crowded dance floor, and the ballroom dances covered in this book are especially challenging because they are not stationary dances—they progress around the floor. In chapter 4, the alignments of the dance floor were explained, but on the social dance floor it might seem almost impossible to follow those directions. There will always be dancers who do not understand the alignments, so someone who has taken lessons has the advantage. Properly maneuvering around the dance floor is called *floorcraft*, and good floorcraft not only makes the dancing enjoyable, it also ensures safety for all concerned.

The easiest thing to remember is that most of the time you should travel on diagonals—zigzagging along the line of dance. The direction of your turn should also be determined by the direction you are facing on the dance floor. If you are facing diagonal center, you have to turn to the left. If you're facing diagonal wall, you turn to the right. The only exception is dancing the Viennese waltz. When turning to the left you should be facing either line of dance or diagonal wall, and when turning to the right you should be facing line of dance or diagonal center. To turn to the left, your left foot has to move forward, and to turn to the right, your right foot has to move forward. Moving in this way will help you maneuver around the other dancers who are also moving. One of the biggest mistakes new dancers make is thinking that the dance floor is static. They plan where to go based on the position of the dancers at a given moment, forgetting that even in one second, the floor will change. The woman can often see what's going on behind the man, and if there will be a collision with another couple, she can signal him by stopping her own body from moving or just by using her left hand to stop him. In dance position, the lady's left hand should be on the man's right arm.

> **N**o matter what teachers of dancing may assert, the most expedient and certainly the best way to learn to dance is to stand up and try it; no one can ever learn by sitting quietly and looking on.
>
> *From* Wilson's Ball-Room Guide and Call Book *by George E. Wilson*
> *(New York: Excelsior Publishing House, 1884)*

If the dance floor is especially crowded, be aware of the movements of the other dancers, and don't try to push other dancers out of your way. The best thing to do is the same thing you would do on a crowded freeway. The driver that cuts off other cars is not the most popular driver on the road and creates potentially hazardous conditions. Likewise, "daredevil dancers" are not likely to be the most popular dancers. A lady does not feel safe dancing with a partner who dances this way and uses her as a battering ram. Remember this key point: instead of dancing offensively, practice defensive (yet confident) dancing. Be aware of the space you are occupying as a couple.

Often, competition or exhibition dancers enjoy social dancing as well. However, it's considered bad form to practice specially choreographed routines on the social dance floor. Usually, competition-style dancing and routines meant for performance include large arm movements or step patterns that may be too static. Sometimes they may even include theatrical movements, such as aerials (where one partner lifts the other partner off the floor) or drops (where one partner sits or lies on the floor). Those can be dangerous to other couples, especially to beginners just experiencing the trials of line of dance with others on the floor for the first time. But if no one else is dancing and a couple is on the floor alone, it may be okay to show off a bit. They just need to be smart about it. It's important for everyone to be aware of their surroundings and considerate of other dancers, for their own safety and the safety of others.

When you can maneuver your way around the floor successfully and in a safe and effortless manner, you will truly understand the joys of partner dancing. The dances we have covered in this book each have built-in evasive steps, or steps used to avoid dangerous situations or potential collisions with other couples. Each dance has its own feel and style, and the way it progresses around the floor may feel different because of this. Recognizing the differences and understanding how to use the tools of each dance will help you to enjoy the dances more fully.

Waltz is probably the most difficult dance to maneuver because it rotates as it moves down the line. Sometimes dancers do the box steps without turning or turning only a quarter of a turn. This lack of progression around the floor causes traffic jams. At a public dance, those patterns should be used only in corners. They are taught mainly as tools to better understand the box step pattern and to coordinate the body movements as you learn how to turn. Gradually, the body becomes more coordinated and can make the whole three-eighths turn on each 1, 2, 3, which enables you to move along the line of dance. Other waltz step patterns in this book that move you down the line of dance are the forward progressive basic, side by side progressive basic, and grapevine. The hesitations—forward, backward, and side—are evasive step patterns that enable you to avoid running into another couple.

Of all the ballroom dances, tango is probably the easiest to move around the floor. Walking steps can always be added to the beginning of almost any pattern in order to move away from other dancers. The walks can be straight ahead or curved to the left, but there has to be an even number—left, right— because all of the step patterns start with the left foot for the man. The tango step patterns that move down the line of dance are promenade, tango rocks, left turn, and left turn with fan. Step patterns used to avoid other couples are simple corte, double corte turning, and curving the forward walking steps to change the direction you are moving.

Most of the foxtrot step patterns move down the line of dance in a zigzag pattern (see figure 10.3). The turning basic and grapevine are the most prominent zigzag patterns. The promenade step pattern moves down the line of dance. The evasive steps are chasse and left turn. They should be used to turn a corner or to change direction to get away from another couple.

Like waltz, Viennese waltz is a little more difficult to keep moving down the line of dance because of the turning movements. If couples do not make the complete turn, they will cause traffic jams. That's when other dancers usually use the hesitation patterns, but then the couples that hesitate add to the traffic problem. The better you understand how to turn the Viennese waltz, the more you will be able to get around the obstacles without causing traffic problems for other dancers.

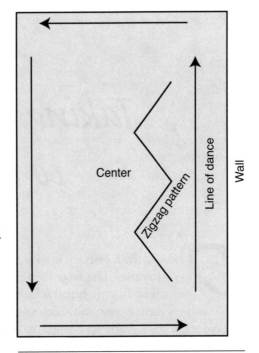

Figure 10.3 Moving down the line of dance in a zigzag pattern.

Most important, remember to enjoy the experience of your first dance and all the dances that follow. Have fun with whatever happens. You're still learning. Each dance will get easier and will bring more confidence.

11

Taking Your Dancing to the Next Level

Dancing has gotten into your blood and you're ready for more. What now? The next step is to decide how deeply you want to get involved in this hobby. Some people go out dancing infrequently, while others dance every day. Some people start out as social dancers, then later decide they want to compete. And still others don't really know what they want until they start—all they know is that they want to dance. Your level of involvement should be what's comfortable for you. Only you know how much time you want to spend on this new hobby and how much money you want to invest in it.

This chapter answers some of your questions about how to find a dance school and instructor that are right for you and your personal dance goals. Various terms are explained to help you understand the levels of dancing and the types of lessons that are available. Resources for finding social dance clubs in your area are discussed. If your goal is competition, we shed light on the opportunities and requirements for dancing in a competition. This chapter also provides suggestions for joining dance clubs. Supplemental physical activities that you can study to enhance your dancing are introduced.

FINDING AN INSTRUCTOR

Whether it is to be a fun social activity, a competitive sport outlet, or something in between, a high-quality instructor is a must. Depending on where you live, finding a dance teacher can be daunting. If you live in a rural area, you may not have many choices, or you may have to drive some distance. If you live in a large metropolitan area, you may be faced with seemingly countless choices and may not be sure which teacher to choose. The most important thing is to match your interests to the teacher. Do some research. If you are looking for the best, the most expensive may not always be the best. On the other hand, going for the least expensive to save money may cost you more in the long run.

Check out different dance studios and instructors and talk with the students who attend classes there. Many studios offer introductory specials. Usually it's the first two or three lessons at a reduced rate, and if you get lucky, some studios offer your first lesson free. All studios are different. Take advantage of this introductory period to meet other students at the studio and talk to them about their experiences. See how you feel there and how you are treated. Do you like the school? Their hours? The people? The location? Keep in mind that shopping around for a studio is perfectly fine, but if you spend a lot of time trying out 20 different studios, you might find that you've spent quite a bit of money studio hopping and end up not learning much in the end. Because it takes a lesson or two for teachers to assess your dancing aptitude and goals and to plan their approach to teaching you, it's difficult to progress if you are with a new teacher every week. You need continuity in your dance training in order to feel progress. It's best to narrow your initial search to a few studios and instructors.

When you find a teacher you feel comfortable with, talk about his or her training: length of time teaching, dance experience, examination credentials, competition styles he or she has competed in. Finding out whether he or she still takes lessons is also significant, regardless of the level of dancer you want to become. Being a good teacher is directly linked to continuing education. Explain what your interests and goals are. If the teacher and studio are reputable, the teacher will not pressure you into lessons, but instead, answer your questions and give you the time to make your own decisions.

> **F**ind someone whose dancing style appeals to you. It's important that you and your teacher have the same goals. Your teacher should be your role model.
>
> *Michelle Officer, professional American ballroom champion,*
> *Dance Notes, April 1998*

There are several types of dance studios: franchised, such as Arthur Murray Dance Studios and Fred Astaire Dance Studios, and independent. Although most franchised schools are run in a similar fashion around the country, independent studios can vary quite a bit. Former franchise studio owners sometimes open their own independent schools, so they adhere to similar business practices as if they were part of a franchise. When you purchase lessons at a franchise studio, you often buy packages of lessons that will include a block of private lessons, group classes, and practice parties. Some independent studios sell similar packages. At other studios, you purchase everything separately. Neither system is better than the other; they are just different ways of doing business. It used to be that most franchise schools were geared mainly toward social dancers, and independent schools had a reputation for catering to competition students. That's no longer the case. Although it's true that some schools tend to be more oriented toward teaching either social or competition styles of dance, there is much crossover. You can find either style

© Corbis

Arthur Murray, pictured here with wife Kathryn, revolutionized the way people learned to dance as founder of one of the largest franchised dance studio chains in the world.

at either type of school. Make sure you ask up front if the school specializes in one or the other in case your interest is drawn in a particular way.

Let's look at the different types of lessons. A private lesson is a one-on-one session between you and your teacher, or if you have a partner, between you and your partner and your teacher. Even if you have a built-in dance partner (e.g., husband, wife, girlfriend), you may choose to take some lessons with your own instructors as well. That's something you can decide as your learning progresses. Some people find they learn in a more accelerated fashion when they have complete attention on their own dancing, and then they can bring back more to the partnership. Others prefer to experience all of their lessons with their partner. If money is an issue, this might be the best route because you pay for each instructor's time. Sometimes couples will take occasional lessons on their own.

Private lessons can be structured in many ways. Look at why you are taking lessons and your goals. If you are taking lessons to spend quality time with your partner, then lessons together might be what you want. If you desire to compete, then some lessons on your own might be helpful. And remember, you don't need a partner to take private lessons, so don't feel you must search for one before you can start learning. Also know that a private lesson does not necessarily mean that you will be in a private room. It just means that you will have one instructor completely focused on you for the entire session. Depending on the size of the studio, you may share the floor with many other students having private lessons as well. You may be learning one dance while others are learning a different dance just a few feet away. Although this may sound like it would be confusing, it really isn't. You will find that you become completely involved with what you are doing, and although you are aware of each other's presence, you go about doing your own thing. During the course of a private lesson, you will usually divide your time between several dances. However, if you are preparing for a showcase, a special event, or a competition, you will most likely concentrate on your upcoming event.

Group lessons are exactly that: lessons in a group. A group class can consist of anywhere from a few people to 20 or even 100. But most classes will probably consist of 10 to 20 students. During a group class there is usually one instructor for the entire class, but sometimes there may be an assistant, especially in larger classes. Usually, just one dance will be covered, but sometimes in longer sessions the time may be split between two dances. Be aware that in most group classes, everyone usually dances with nearly everyone else. The instructor will periodically have everyone switch partners. It's rare that you stay with the same partner through the entire class, but it depends on how the instructor structures the class.

Some people use group classes to augment their private instruction, while others take one or the other exclusively. Group lessons are an added way to maximize your dancing experience without spending a lot of money because they usually cost less than private instruction. Again, look around to find teachers that you feel comfortable with and who have the knowledge to teach. Most beginners find learning with a group of people to be fun. It also is a way to meet people who have the same interests and are at the same level of dance. If part of the reason you are taking dance lessons is for more social interaction, then group classes may be just the ticket. Some beginners feel more comfortable with private lessons first, then when they gain confidence, they go into group classes. Some prefer to do it the other way around; they join a group class and get a few basics down, then pursue private instruction.

All the students in a group class are usually at the same level of learning, but those levels may be broad. The instructor will try to gear the lesson to the median level of the group. If you learn quicker than most, you may get bored or feel that the class is too slow. If you learn more slowly, you may feel that you can't keep up. The teacher should try to keep everyone moving along at a comfortable pace. You generally learn faster with private instruction than with group instruction because the lesson is geared specifically to you and your method of learning. You set the pace. The teacher will give you information as quickly as you are able to absorb it, whereas in a group setting, your pace may not match the other students in the class.

If you are serious about your dancing, then private lessons are a must, but they can be expensive. If competition is a goal, then you definitely need private instruction with an instructor who also competes or has competed professionally. Competing professionals tend to be a little more serious about the dancing and will teach a lot of detailed technique. Generally, teachers who have never competed tend to gear their lessons more toward the social dancer. That's fine, of course, but if you want to compete, you may need and desire more. Understand that these are sweeping statements and there are always exceptions, but on the whole, competing professionals understand the

competition world because they have experienced it. Whether for social dancing or competition dancing, private lessons from high-quality instructors can
be somewhat expensive, comparable to the cost of golf or tennis lessons from
a professional. But remember that you are paying for a specialized service
from a trained professional. The duration of a private or group class varies
depending on the policies and procedures of the studio and instructor. Lessons can last anywhere from 30 minutes to two hours, but the average and
most used increments for dance lessons (both group and private) are 40 to
45 or 50 to 55 minutes. Make certain you understand the pricing structure
and policies of your studio or independent instructor.

Most dance studios, along with private and group lessons, offer practice
sessions or studio dances. They are usually held once a week in the evening,
lasting from two to three hours, but some studios may offer two or even three
parties a week. Dance parties are a great way to enhance your lesson experience
in a comfortable atmosphere. During these parties, you have the opportunity
to dance with other students who are just beginning, more advanced students,
and even instructors. Use this time to experience dancing with a variety of
partners. If you make mistakes, it's okay. Everyone is there to learn and have
fun, so remember to enjoy it. It's not a test!

Most dance studios also hold a function once or twice a year called a
showcase. A showcase is like a dance recital, and may be held in the studio
if it is large enough, or sometimes in another facility, such as a hotel ballroom. A showcase gives the students an opportunity to perform the dances
they are learning. These routines, which are usually choreographed by your
instructor, are done at any level—even beginning dancers can do a showcase
routine. Sometimes they are judged and other times the shows are just for
enjoyment. If they are judged, they are usually not judged like a competition.
You will be critiqued against a standard of dancing based on your level, and
usually you will be given comments from the adjudicator that will help you
in your future learning. The great thing about participation in a showcase is
that it can accelerate your progress. You help yourself by working specifically.
If you know that you need to perfect a dance by a certain date, you will work
a little harder toward that end. If you are shy about performing, don't worry.
You will never be forced to do a showcase. It is just another tool that is there
for you if you want it. Even if you don't dance in one at the beginning, go and
watch others dance. You can garner a lot of information from watching, and
you might find that you have a great time as well.

PROFICIENCY LEVELS OF DANCE

You'll discover that the dance world has a whole new language, but most
studios and teachers use similar terminology. There are two styles of ballroom
dance—American and international. The two styles are subdivided even further
into American ballroom (or smooth) and American rhythm, and international
standard and international Latin. Roughly, American ballroom is comparable

to the international standard and the American rhythm is comparable to the international Latin. Let's look at some of the similarities and differences.

American style is danced mostly in the United States, but other countries are now adopting their own versions of it. International style is danced the same all over the world. The step patterns are the same whether danced in the United States, Europe, China, or Australia. In American style, the step patterns may be different from one city to another, one franchise to another, or even between two studios down the street from each other! The reason for this is that there is no world standardization of the step patterns as there is in the international style. There are several organizations that have standardized the American style to some extent, and many studios opt to use a step syllabus suggested by one of these organizations. The step patterns, however, are merely the tools through which you learn how to dance. By learning the proper way to dance, even if the actual steps are different, you can still dance with others who did not take lessons at the same place you did. The steps don't really matter. The technique learned is what enables you to dance with anyone.

> **O**ne of the most important things is that teachers communicate clearly and that they primarily teach in principles. A teaching principle is something that the student can take away from the lesson and apply to every single action that is similar.
>
> *Edward Simon, professional American ballroom champion,*
> Dance Notes, *April 1998*

In American ballroom (the style covered in this book), the most common dances are the waltz, tango, foxtrot, and Viennese waltz. The international standard adds one more dance: the quickstep. Even though the dances are essentially similar and there are a good number of step patterns that can be danced in either style, the styles differ drastically in one major way. The American ballroom style allows more room for interpretation, meaning that the partners sometimes separate for a turn or some other type of apart movement, while in the international standard, the couple never separates or steps out of dance hold. The actual dance technique, however, is the same. The international Latin dances are the cha cha, rumba, samba, paso doble, and jive. The American rhythm dances generally include the cha cha, rumba, swing, bolero, and mambo. The basic ideology of the international Latin and American rhythm is similar, but the techniques vary. You will find that American and international rumba, for example, are very different dances.

The dances mentioned thus far are the basic dances that are taught in all four styles for social dancers and are the basis for most competitions. However, although the international style stays strictly with the 10 dances mentioned previously, the American style can be opened up to include many more dances, both for the competitive and the social dancer. In American ballroom, the Peabody is sometimes danced, and in American rhythm we often see the hustle, merengue, salsa, samba, and others.

What are reasons for choosing one style over the other? Some students enjoy the freedom and room for expression that American ballroom offers, while others choose international standard for the discipline and solid technical basis gained. Even American ballroom dancers will often study international standard to gain a stronger understanding of the technique. If your goal is to be strictly a social dancer, American style ballroom and rhythm will give you more variety. However, depending on where you live, international style may be danced socially, so ask around. If you want to compete, you will be afforded the same opportunities in both American and international, at least in the United States. Also, when selecting your instructor and studio, find out if they offer (or specialize) in one style or the other, or if they teach all styles.

Even though we are only covering the four American ballroom dances in this book, the reason we mention all of these styles and dances is to give you a general understanding of what you may encounter when you want to advance your dancing. Some people prefer only American style, while others prefer only international. Some do a little of each, and still others do it all. Again, it depends on your goals, your time, your budget, and your level of commitment. If you are only taking one private lesson a week, trying to spread yourself too thin between all the styles will be too much. Be realistic about what you want and how you can get there. Your instructor can help you decide as well. Remember, even if you want to do it all, you don't have to do it all today.

There are three basic levels of learning within each style: bronze, silver, and gold. Bronze is the beginning level, silver is the intermediate level, and gold is an advanced level. Some teachers and studios also teach levels above gold. They are called open gold and gold star.

In the American style, the bronze is the first level of dancing, and everyone starts at this level. The patterns and techniques at this level teach you to be a very good social dancer. This is where you learn dancing with a partner, leading and following, body alignment, movement, footwork, rhythm, timing, rise and fall, sway, and floorcraft—the basic techniques of all the dances. It is important for your future dancing to take your time and study the basics fully. The basics are like the foundation of a house; if the foundation is good and strong, the house can stand, but if the foundation is weak, the house falls down. So the bronze level sets the groundwork for your dancing future. Serious dancers stay at the bronze level for about two years, but that depends on the ability of the person and how many lessons they attend. A good teacher will not rush students through this, but will adjust to the individual's pace of learning. If you want to compete or perform, don't feel that you have to rush through this level. There are competitions at the bronze level. You must make certain to take the time to build a strong base because the more advanced patterns and techniques build on the techniques acquired in the bronze level.

Silver is the second level. These dancers can be hobby dancers or very serious competitors. At this level, dancers are beginning to move toward the standard of dancing you see in professional performances, which means they are using open footwork and other intricate techniques. Silver dancers have gone through all the basic techniques at the bronze level and are now studying the more advanced technical aspects of dancing. The step patterns are more intricate and showy. A deeper understanding of the body movements and dance position is developed. A silver-level dancer usually practices dancing at least twice a week to gain proficiency. As a competitor, a dancer at this level often goes to many competitions and appreciates the competition route.

Gold is the third level of dancing. A dancer who achieves this level is extremely proficient and would, in most cases, be a high-level competitor. Sometimes, students who have no wish to compete will dance at this level simply because of their love of dancing. They enjoy learning about themselves and the dancing, so they continue taking lessons indefinitely. The intricate step patterns learned in the gold level require a solid background. These patterns are generally not used on a crowded ballroom floor, but reserved for competitions, exhibition dancing, and performances. Even if you want to be a gold-level dancer, the teacher always starts the student at the bronze level, and the dancer works his or her way up through the ranks. Think of it this way: Let's say that bronze is high school, silver is college, and gold is graduate school. You can't go to graduate school until you get your undergraduate degree, and you can't go to college until you earn your high school diploma and the knowledge that it brings.

There are various ways to go from one level to the next, and it depends on your teacher or the studio. Some teachers just decide on their own when to move their students up. This is often the case in independent studios, or when the instructor is not affiliated with a particular studio. If you take lessons at a large studio, sometimes a dance director from the studio gives tests, and there may even be a graduation-like ceremony to reward the students who have passed. In addition, examiners travel around the country and test students out of each level. The tests usually include dancing some of the step patterns by yourself, answering basic questions, and dancing with a partner. If your studio doesn't offer a standardized test, then your instructor will let you know when you are ready to move up. Be honest with your instructor regarding your goals, and he or she will help design a program to make those goals achievable. You can move as slowly or as quickly through the levels as you want.

COMPETITION DANCING

Competition dancing is an excellent way to improve rapidly and have a great time. Competing gives you a goal, which makes you study and prepare much harder. There are various levels and age categories that you can compete in, so anyone at any level or age can be a competition dancer. If you do not have a partner, you can even dance with your instructor, which is called the pro–am division. If you have a partner, you would compete in the amateur division. Professional divisions are for dancers who have made ballroom dancing their career.

You can attend various types of competitions. The USA Dance organization sponsors competitions all over the country for amateur dancers. Dancers can start at 6 years old in the junior division. Categories go up through the senior division, which can include dancers 80 years old and even older. Levels at events include bronze, silver, gold, and open gold. Most of these competitions have scholarship divisions also, and students can win money for dance lessons.

The National Dance Council of America (NDCA) also runs dance competitions. They are similar to the USA Dance events, but their competitions can include pro-am and professional divisions. A pro-am couple is a student dancing with his or her teacher, who is a professional. The professional division is two pros dancing together. The pro-am divisions have age categories and levels similar to those in the USA Dance competitions. There are also male and female categories, so you always compete against other students who are at the same level and of the same age and gender. The professional competitions provide an exciting and entertaining show for the other competition participants. Somewhere in the United States there is at least one NDCA dance competition every weekend.

If competition dancing is your goal, there are many costs to consider: costumes, entry fees, teacher fees, extra lessons, travel expenses, etc. You must buy or rent a special dance costume, which can be very elaborate and expensive. The ladies dresses will have many layers of fabric and thousands of rhinestones glued on them. The men wear specially made dance tuxes or tail suits. Entry fees and travel expenses can vary depending on the size and location of the event. Also, consider that you will have to pay a fee to dance with a professional instruc-

Photo courtesy of Jonathan S. Marion, © 2007

For those wishing to take social dancing to the next level, competition dancing is a fun and challenging way to improve dance skills quickly (pictured here is the Blackpool Dance Festival, one of the most prestigious dance competitions in the world).

tor and take extra lessons to prepare. So, it's best to talk with the studio or instructor about all of the fees and costs involved in being a competition dancer before you take this step. If you want to compete occasionally, that's an option as well. Although some students go to a competition every month, some may compete only once a year.

DANCE CLUBS

If you only want to dance socially, that's fine. There are many opportunities to dance in nightclubs and at singles dances. Most local newspapers list dances and meetings of various organizations. Many areas of the country have organized dance clubs. USA Dance is one of them, but there are others. One of the best places to start dancing is at USA Dance dances. USA Dance is a national organization that promotes ballroom dancing for dancers of all ages and levels. They host dances, workshops, and dance competitions. This association has branches in many cities. At the start of the evening, a beginner group class is often taught by one of the local instructors. The lesson is usually followed by two hours of dancing. It's a great way to meet other dancers and find out about other dances in the area.

> Every day brings a chance for you to draw in a breath, kick off your shoes, and dance.
>
> *Oprah Winfrey*

Singles clubs also hold dances at various times during the year, especially around the holidays. Another good way to find a dance club is to search on the Internet, but one of the best ways to find a good place to dance is through word of mouth. Dancers always have great information on good dancing. A dance club is a great place for people who have the same interests to get together for a nice social evening. The club might have dances once a month or a few times a year. You might get so interested that you want to start one yourself. It doesn't have to be a formal club; it can be just a group of people who enjoy going out dancing together. You never know where you might meet these people. The parents of your children's friends might be interested, or maybe someone you work with or members of another club that you belong to will be interested. You might even find prospects at the grocery store. Many people enjoy getting together with friends in a comfortable atmosphere to dance the night away.

SUPPLEMENTAL PHYSICAL ACTIVITIES

To enhance your dancing, there are other activities that will also educate your body to move more efficiently and will make you feel better even when not dancing. Any activity that involves stretching and developing the body and mind is great for dancing. These are just a few of the many activities that can improve fitness and make your dancing better. To get more information on these practices, check your local library or the Internet.

- Pilates teaches balance and control of the body. Exercises can be done on Pilates machines or on a mat. Among the many benefits are better posture and balance and more flexibility and strength.

- Alexander technique is a study of the correct alignment of the body. Practice of this technique will improve ease and freedom of movement and coordination.

- Another body-enhancing technique developed in the 1940s is the Feldenkrais method. This method uses awareness as a tool to identify and adjust ineffective movement. Many times it is used in conjunction with chiropractic adjustments and massage therapy. Feldenkrais is mainly practiced in a one-on-one situation with the instructor gently guiding the student to explore new ways to move his or her body.

- Yoga is an ancient Indian practice that dates back more than 5,000 years. The three main yoga structures are breathing, exercise, and meditation. Ancient yogis developed this because they believed that for people to be in harmony with themselves and the environment, their mind, body, and spirit had to be integrated. Yoga exercises your mind as well as your body. It improves circulation and stimulates the abdominal organs and glands, which lead to better health.

- Aerobics is a fitness exercise developed in the 1960s and is usually done to music in a class situation. Over the years, many variations of this exercise form have developed, including step aerobics, water aerobics, punk rock aerobics, and even urban striptease aerobics. Aerobics uses repetitive motions of long duration to improve cardiorespiratory fitness, muscular strength, flexibility, and endurance.

- Gyrotonic training, which was created in the 1980s, is done on machines. It combines movements from yoga, tai chi, swimming, and gymnastics. It stimulates cardiac activity and strengthens the connective tissue surrounding the joints.

- Developed in the 1980s, spinning is aerobic exercise on a stationary bike. The instructor plays music and walks the participant through the visualization of a workout. Sometimes participants visualize riding up a hill and working hard, other times they coast. This exercise works the body and also the mind through the visualization aspect.

Studying other dance styles is always beneficial, too. Ballet, tap, jazz, modern, and even hip-hop dancing classes can help you exercise your dance muscles. The technique and discipline acquired through other dance classes help you move your body and get it used to learning and moving like a dancer. You may even find that you can incorporate some of the styling and technique into your ballroom moves.

Whether you decide to be an occasional dancer, a top-level competitor, or something in between, we hope this book and DVD have helped you get started on the right foot toward your goals. As you have seen, ballroom dancing has evolved into an exciting part of our culture and will only continue to grow in popularity. Congratulations on taking this first step into the world of ballroom. Enjoy what you've learned, and keep on ballroom dancing!

Dance Resources

Dance Publications

Dance Notes

In-depth interviews with dancesport personalities
PO Box 30
New York, NY 10028
877-336-6837
www.dancenotes.com

Dance Beat

Dancesport competition results
1172 S. Dixie Hwy, #492
Coral Gables, FL 33146
305-531-3087
www.dancebeat.com

International Dance Directory

PO Box 26277
Minneapolis, MN 55426
612-927-6603
www.dancedirectory.com

North American Dance Almanac

Frank Regan
703-823-2623

Dance Organizations

Imperial Society of Teachers of Dancing—US Branch (USISTD)

www.usistd.org

Arthur Murray Dance Studios

1077 Ponce de Leon Blvd.
Coral Gables, FL 33134
305-445-9645
www.arthurmurray.com

USA Dance

Amateur dance organization
PO Box 152988
Cape Coral, FL 33915-2988
800-447-9047
www.usadance.org

Fred Astaire Franchised Dance Studios

10 Bliss Rd.
Longmeadow, MA 01106
413-567-3200
www.fredastaire.com

Professional Dance Vision International Dance Association

Dance teachers organization
9081 W. Sahara Ave.
Las Vegas, NV 89117
800-851-2813
www.prodvida.com

National Dance Council of America

Governing body for dance in the United States
Mr. Lee Wakefield
PO Box 22018
Provo, Utah 84602
801-378-5087
www.ndca.org

International DanceSport Federation

www.idsf.net

Dancewear

Designs by Lyn

Women's dancewear
Lyn Wallander
239-332-5442
www.designsbylyn.com

Dee's Creations

Rental and made-to-order dance dresses
Dee Michael
410-583-8870
deescreations@groups.msn.com

Deirdre of London

Dance dresses
Deirdre Baker
561-966-6160
www.deirdreoflondon.com

DancePants

Men's dancewear
408-363-8393
www.dancepants.com

Onik, Tailor of the Champions

Men's tail suits, tuxedos, and Latin costumes
213-380-3272
www.dancewearformen.com

Donna Inc., Artistic Dancesport Designs by Donna Hamza

Dance dresses
302-322-1993
donnahamza@aol.com

Burkhart's Best Foot Forward

Dance shoes
610-926-1918
www.dance-shoes-gallery.com

Ballroom Etcetera

Dance accessories
502-891-0994
www.ballroometc.com

Be-Dazzled

Jewelry and accessories
414-352-2557
bedazzld@yahoo.com

Doré Exquisite Gowns

Dance costumes
239-542-7708
www.dore-designs.com

LeNique

Men's and women's designer dancewear
310-246-9390
www.LeNique.com

Randall Designs

Men's and women's dancewear
562-438-7788
www.randalldesigns.net

Showtime Dance Shoes

Ballroom and Latin dance shoes
800-433-5541
www.showtimedanceshoes.com

Capezio Dance Shoes

Men's and women's dance shoes
Ben Pignataro
bpignataro@balletmakers.com
www.capeziodance.com

Chrisanne

Practice wear and competition dresses
706-579-0460
ivy@chrisanne.us
www.chrisanne.com

Danz2000

Dance shoes
917-681-9761
www.danz2000.com

Ron Gunn Tailors

International and American dancewear for men
398 Lea Bridge Rd.
Leyton, London E10 7DY
United Kingdom
011-44-208-539-7075
011-44-208-539-7076 (fax)

General Dance Resources

Dance Partner Finder
www.dancepartner.com

Dancing Art
Original art and prints
615-627-1080
800-716-0080
www.dancingart.com

Dance Vision
Videotapes, DVDs, and CDs
800-851-2813
www.dancevision.com

Glamour Puss
Dancesport hair and makeup
Lisa Bentley
302-438-2890
www.glamrpuss.com

Dancescape
866-309-6470
www.dancescape.com

Pro Dance
Music and videos
800-992-9282

Dance Forums
Online message boards with dance information
www.dance-forums.com

American Dance Wheels Foundation
Support for and promotion of wheelchair dancing
Melinda Kremer or Ray Leight
www.americandancewheels.org
215 588-6671

Dance-Related Resources

SFS Kids: Fun With Music
Music identification and rhythm program from the San Francisco Symphony
www.sfskids.org

Music and Rhythm Games
www.ababasoft.com/music

Alexander Technique
www.Alexandertechnique.com

Feldenkrais Method
www.feldenkrais.com

Yoga
www.yoga.com

Spinning
www.spinning.com

Aerobics
www.aboutaerobics.com

Gyrotonics
www.gyrotonics.com

About the Authors

Christine Zona is a former ballroom studio owner and competitor. She has danced professionally in the international standard and Latin divisions and in the American ballroom division and won several Rising Star titles. She is a certified teacher and adjudicator in American ballroom and rhythm, international standard and Latin, and theatre arts divisions and is a member of many professional dance organizations. Currently, she judges ballroom dance competitions, instructs dancers of all ages, and is the editor of *Dance Notes*, a national bimonthly publication devoted to ballroom dance (www.dancenotes.com). Zona resides in New York City.

Chris George is a professional ballroom dancer, teacher, and former competitor. He has competed in the American ballroom and rhythm divisions, winning a number of Rising Star titles. He is a former coeditor of *Dance Notes* and now serves as a contributing editor. Currently pursuing a career on stage as an actor, singer, and dancer, he has danced at the internationally renowned Moulin Rouge in Paris and performed on two national tours of the Broadway shows *Kiss Me, Kate* and *The Full Monty*. George resides in New York City.